THE PURPOSE-DRIVEN
INFLUENCER

A Soulful Guide To Authentic Living & Leading From The Heart

THE PURPOSE-DRIVEN
INFLUENCER

A Soulful Guide to Authentic Living & Leading From the Heart

Jimmy Jean

AUTHOR ACADEMY elite

The Purpose-Driven Influencer © 2025 by Jimmy Jean. All rights reserved.

Published by Author Academy Elite
PO Box 43, Powell, OH 43065

IgnitingSouls.com

All rights reserved. No part of this publication may be reproduced, distributed, or transmitted in any form or by any means, including photocopying, recording, or other electronic or mechanical methods, without the prior written permission of the publisher, except in the case of brief quotations embodied in critical reviews and certain other noncommercial uses permitted by copyright law.

LCCN: 2024901024
ISBN: 979-8-88583-324-0 (paperback)
ISBN: 979-8-88583-325-7 (hardback)
ISBN: 979-8-88583-326-4 (ebook)

Available in paperback, hardback, e-book, and audiobook.

Unless otherwise indicated, all Scripture quotations are from The ESV® Bible (The Holy Bible, English Standard Version®), copyright © 2001 by Crossway, a publishing ministry of Good News Publishers. Used by permission. All rights reserved.

Any Internet addresses (websites, blogs, etc.) and telephone numbers printed in this book are offered as a resource. They are not intended in any way to be or imply an endorsement by Author Academy Elite, nor does Author Academy Elite vouch for the content of these sites and numbers for the life of this book.

Contents

Foreword	1
Introduction	5
PART ONE: A Higher Calling	17
1. Becoming A Purpose-Driven Influencer	19
2. It's Not About You	27
3. Build Your Inner Brand	51
PART TWO - The Making Of An Influencer	71
4. Purpose Over Popularity	73
5. You Are Verified	93
PART THREE: Your Path To Elevation	113
6. Run Your Own Race	115
7. Alignment Is The New Hustle	137
A Moment Of Gratitude	181
Endnotes	183

STAY CONNECTED

Instagram: @TheRoadToPurpose
Website: JimmyJean.com

Foreword

In the bustling heart of New York City, amid the towering skyscrapers and the constant hum of urban life, I met a young man whose impact would resonate with me for over two decades. His name is Jimmy Jean, a radiant soul whose journey from guest service agent at the London NY (formerly RIHGA Royal) to the author of this inspiring book, "The Purpose Driven Influencer," is nothing short of remarkable.

For twenty years, my broadcast partner, Tim Brando, and I were welcomed by Jimmy's warm smile every time we entered the hotel lobby. In that time, I witnessed a peaceful passion emanating from him—a passion born out of agency and gratitude.

This profound outlook on life has not wavered; Jimmy continues to possess a strong heart for serving and inspiring others to lead purposeful lives. The pages of this book offer a glimpse into the lens through which he sees the world and the transformative power of living with intention.

Jimmy's personal story unfolds like an archetypal narrative that Hollywood has thrived on—the hero's journey. Starting as an ordinary man leading a relatively commonplace life, he received a call to step into uncharted territory.

The challenge, a seemingly simple request to address his church youth group, unfolded into a commitment far more daunting than he had anticipated. However, along this challenging path, he found a guiding light in the form of Miss Barbara, a mentor who helped him shape his message.

There's a universal truth embedded in Jimmy's journey, reminiscent of the Latin phrase "In Sterquiliniis Invenitur," which translates to "in the filth it shall be found."

This profound saying captures the essence of willfully confronting our deepest fears and challenges. As Jimmy faced his fears on that pivotal day of speaking to his churches' youth group, something magical happened. It was in that moment of confronting the unimaginable that he discovered the seeds of his purpose.

Jimmy's desire to inspire others and guide them on their journey of self-discovery was born from this transformative experience. I sensed a profound purpose within him—an intuition that there were greater things for him to accomplish in this world. His journey began, shaping his life, defining his work, and cultivating a purpose-driven existence.

"The Purpose Driven Influencer" is not just a book; it's a testament to the transformative power of confronting one's fears and embracing a purpose-driven life. Jimmy Jean taps into the generative voice that breathes life into those hungry for more—more meaning, more impact, and more purpose. His words resonate with authenticity, drawing readers into a narrative that transcends the pages and speaks directly to the heart.

As you embark on this journey with Jimmy, be prepared to be challenged, inspired, and moved.

Through his eloquent storytelling and profound insights, he invites you to explore the depths of your own purpose, nudging you towards a life that goes beyond the ordinary. This book is not just a guide; it's a companion for those seeking clarity, purpose, and a path to becoming influencers in their own right.

In a world filled with noise and distractions, "The Purpose Driven Influencer" stands as a beacon of light, reminding us all that our stories, no matter how ordinary they may seem, hold the power to inspire, influence, and shape the lives of others. Thank you, Jimmy Jean, for sharing your journey and inviting us all to discover the purpose that lies within us.

May this book spark a transformative journey for each reader, just as your story has done for me over these past twenty years.

Introduction

"The people who are crazy enough to think they can change the world are the ones that do."

—— Steve Jobs

Our social media platforms are overflowing with influencers. The term "influencer" has become a common presence. It seems as though everyone these days lays claim to that title, and every bio on various platforms proudly displays it. "Influencer" or "Digital Creator" is the catchword of our digital universe. But here's the truth: not all influencers are equal. As I like to say, *"Many Influencers are called, but few have chosen the path of purpose."* Not all are driven by a genuine desire to serve, to leverage their talents and gifts to make the lives of others better.

Many have assumed the title without understanding the weight of responsibility that it carries and what sets purpose-driven influencers apart from the rest.

> MANY INFLUENCERS ARE CALLED, BUT FEW HAVE CHOSEN THE PATH OF PURPOSE.

Purpose-driven influencers operate from a deeper wellspring of motivation. Their mission is not about amassing followers, chasing celebrity status, or seeking fleeting fame and popularity. Instead, their focus is on their ability to inspire and uplift others. Their art, or content, on platforms like Facebook, Twitter, Instagram, or blogs, is not just about aesthetics or shallow engagement. It's about the spirit of purpose that fuels their creative endeavors.

I don't know where you stand on your influencer journey. Perhaps you're experiencing a conflict within yourself, maybe that's why you've picked up this book. You understand that purpose is the true north, yet the temptations of social media - the glitter and allure, the race for recognition, titles, and the need to keep up with peers in the same creative space - have led you astray. You might find yourself trading meaning for metrics, purpose for popularity, and legacy for likes. And let me be perfectly transparent here, I'm not exempt from these struggles. Even the person writing these words has veered off course at times. But if we're to truly create the type of positive change that sends ripples across the globe, it's time for a shift. The same shift I've experienced personally and a shift I believe is imminent for many of us.

You have the power to make that shift, to become the beacon of what real influence and genuine impact should look like when the right intentions and a higher purpose collide. I understand that I'm asking you to do something that might seem uncommon and unpopular, but I believe you can be the change, the purpose-driven influencer you were meant to be.

My deepest aspiration with this book is to inspire all those who have a message to share, to do it the right way—the purpose-driven influencer way. If you've already embraced this identity, my hope is that you find renewed alignment and a stronger commitment to your calling. And every day you log in to your social media accounts, every post you make, every piece of content you share, every time you show up for your followers, you are making a difference, even if the feedback you receive doesn't always reflect that. I see you, your followers see you, and people are inspired by what you have to offer, whether they express it or not. Someone right now has been watching your journey and they are inspired by you and you don't even know it. Whether you're just starting your journey or you're well into it, I'm thrilled you've picked up this book. I'm excited to accompany you on this influencer journey because the world is waiting for the manifestation of purpose-driven influencers to lead the way in this digital age.

In life, some moments become turning points that push you towards your destiny. You may not recognize them at the time, but I hope that as you read my story, you'll begin to see these moments that have already happened for you. Your life experiences so far have been a map, providing miraculous directions towards everything you are supposed to achieve. All you need to do is learn to listen to your inner guidance. As the author, Parker J. Palmer beautifully put it; *"Before I can tell my life what I want to do with it, I must listen to my life telling me who I am".*

My purpose was revealed in an unexpected revelation. It would be my greatest honor if you could allow my story to light the way to your own. Let's begin with one ordinary, yet extraordinary, event from my youth...

> YOUR LIFE EXPERIENCES SO FAR HAVE BEEN A MAP, PROVIDING MIRACULOUS DIRECTIONS TOWARDS EVERYTHING YOU ARE SUPPOSED TO ACHIEVE. ALL YOU NEED TO DO IS LEARN TO LISTEN TO YOUR INNER GUIDANCE.

It all started with a call from a dear friend, Virgil, who was the president of our church's youth group. Virgil, with his infectious enthusiasm, asked me to speak to our youth group during their weekly Sunday meet-ups. My initial reaction was an automatic rejection, rooted in the intense fear of public speaking. But, that infectious enthusiasm worked its magic, and after weeks of gentle persuasion, I apprehensively agreed. Comforted by the knowledge that it would only be a few people from the youth group, the majority friends of mine, I realized there wasn't much to fear at all. What I didn't know is the events that were about to unfold would propel me onto a journey of self-discovery and purpose-driven living.

I was determined to be completely prepared for this unexpected challenge, so I reached out to Barbara, one of our youth leaders. She became my guiding light, helping me craft my first sermon and soothing the nerves of a terrified teenager. Her encouragement and assurance planted a seed of confidence in me. However, as fate would have it, Virgil dropped the ultimate bombshell right at the day of reckoning dawned. The small gathering I had convinced myself was nothing to fear had transformed into a congregation-filled event. I remember our conversation as though it was yesterday; *"You can't be serious right now man?!"* I yelled, panic setting in and nerves going into overdrive. But as that anxiety surged through my body, it activated something I could have never foreseen. A sense of purpose emerged and lit a fire in my belly that burned the memory vividly onto my very Soul...

The speaker introduced me; *"And now we are going to have Jimmy Jean with the message of the night."* As I walked up to the pulpit, the entire congregation was quiet. If my nerves were pins you would have heard them drop all over the place. All I could think was, even if the sermon is terrible, they are not going to boo me in the house of God. That would be sacrilegious. I decided to let that fire burning inside of me to help drive me to deliver the sermon, ironically about overcoming adversity. To my shock and surprise, the room erupted in applause. That day marked not just a successful speaking engagement, but the realization of my reason for walking this Earth. My purpose. That single experience showed me that it is your authenticity that is the biggest influencer. It's being real with yourself, honest with your feelings, emotions, and fears, and seeing each moment that life presents you with as an opportunity to find out what you're capable of. I wanted everyone to share this realization, and from that seed, a calling blossomed. My desire to inspire others and help them on their journey to discovering who they were created to be was born. I sensed a deep feeling of purpose, a subtle intuition that there were greater things for me to accomplish in this world. It was the beginning of a journey that would shape my life, define my work, and cultivate a purpose-driven existence.

You Are The Author Of Your Life

Although I am firmly grounded in purpose now, my journey didn't start that way.

My upbringing unfolded in a volatile environment marked by my father's abuse, both toward my mother and alcohol. The first time I witnessed the brutality up close, I was just five years old. I remember a Sunday when my mother, determined to take me to church, found herself entangled in a shouting match with my father. As I waited in the kitchen for us to leave, the confrontation escalated. He stormed into the bedroom with a broom in his hand. The echoes of my mother's pain reverberated through the house as she endured the beating. All I could do was sit there, powerless, tears streaming down my face. Church became a distant memory, as my mother was too battered to accompany me.

My relationship with my father was distant, to say the least, I felt rejected and out of place, especially when I noticed other kids lucky enough to have both their parents at school events. Life at home was tough, and I had to grow up quickly to protect my mom and sisters from my father's anger. Amidst the chaos and trauma at home, high school became a struggle. The unpredictability of returning home felt burdensome, making it difficult to concentrate on studies. Living amidst my parents' fights, school became a secondary concern, leading me to engage in self-sabotaging behaviors, like playing hooky. The consequences caught up, and eventually, a pivotal phone call from my high school shattered my world. My mother was called in to sign the papers which meant I would no longer be a student at the school. The ride home was filled with tears and disappointment. I had hit rock bottom. Even though we were all heartbroken, and the situation raw, my mom insisted that I self-reflect immediately. She wanted me to make something of myself and she understood that this crossroads was a crucial time in which I could either cement my rock bottom or start the climb to the top. She was right, and I chose to enroll in GED classes. This marked the beginning of my healing journey and against the odds, led to college.

Slowly, my mom began to heal too, and as we both started to grow, I realized that your background and circumstances may have played a role in who you are, but it does not have a say on who you have the potential to become. Leaving an abusive situation is hard, but my mom eventually found the courage to do it. This decision and the strength she found within brought us closer together as a family, and she became a role model for me on which to find my own inner strength. We faced tough times as a single-parent family and I learned important lessons from our mom about resilience and hard work.

As positive changes took root, I made a promise to myself that I would become a messenger of purpose, driven by the desire to ensure no one feels like a failure. I was taught that what you go through is never for you, it's for that person that you will encounter on your journey who will need the wisdom of your story to help them on their path. I am proof that you can write a new story. No matter

> I REALIZED THAT YOUR BACKGROUND AND CIRCUMSTANCES MAY HAVE PLAYED A ROLE IN WHO YOU ARE, BUT IT DOES NOT HAVE A SAY ON WHO YOU HAVE THE POTENTIAL TO BECOME.

how bad it seems, you have the power to turn everything into gold. So wherever you are on your journey, you can decide right now, that this is not how your story ends. You didn't go through all that you've been through to just persevere and not progress. I was once told never to place a period where God has placed a comma. You have to keep going because your best days are still ahead of you. It has been said; *"when the student is ready, the teacher will appear"*. Every time I have been at a crossroads in my life, the right person has appeared to help and guide me through. It's thanks to these divinely sent mentors that I began my personal development journey. If you look back at some of the most pivotal moments of your life, I'm willing to bet you'll be able to spot your own mentors.

God knew I needed some divine guidance because my mother was juggling so many responsibilities. But she believed in me, and running on that borrowed belief, my life began to change, and I became a better version of myself. It was CS Lewis who said; *"Hardships often prepare ordinary people for an extraordinary destiny"*. No matter who you are, no matter what you've been through, you have the power to take back the pen from the abusers, the doubters, and naysayers, and write a new beautiful story of healing and victory that transforms your mess into your message.

> NO MATTER WHO YOU ARE, NO MATTER WHAT YOU'VE BEEN THROUGH, YOU HAVE THE POWER TO TAKE BACK THE PEN FROM THE ABUSERS, THE DOUBTERS, AND NAYSAYERS, AND WRITE A NEW BEAUTIFUL STORY OF HEALING AND VICTORY THAT TRANSFORMS YOUR MESS INTO YOUR MESSAGE.

Answer The Call

I remember the moment when I felt the urge to write this book. I had wanted to write for a long time, but the message hadn't yet become clear. I tried a few times, but nothing felt right until now. Sometimes you have to wait for the book to come to you. This is true of any calling that might show up for you in life. You have to make space for it. You can not force divine ideas, you have to be open to receiving them.

One night, in the quiet darkness of my living room, the idea for this book hit me. I was thinking about my purpose and the dream of writing a book. The title just came to me – *"The Purpose-Driven Influencer."* I was excited, but then I immediately doubted myself. That little voice in your head can be your worst critic.

Even with fears and doubts, the idea kept nudging me, and I knew I had to ignore that inner naysayer. Signs for me to write this book appeared in various ways. I even had the phrase *"Purpose-Driven Influencer"* on my Instagram bio before I knew it would be my book title.

It's not just a title, it's a statement about why I'm here. Purpose-driven influencers operate on a higher frequency. We're not better; we just have a different mission. So here I am, saying yes to telling my story and serving a new generation of influencers who want to make a difference authentically.

For a long time, I looked for a guide for influencers like me, but I couldn't find it. Then I remembered a quote by Toni Morrison: *"If there is a book you want to read, but it hasn't been written yet, then you must write it."* Purpose-driven influencers create what they wish existed. I hope that you answer your own personal call and say yes to whatever you are being led to create. Life is always speaking to you in tiny whispers intended to gently move you in the direction of your destiny. The trick is to create stillness so that you can listen. So my first invitation to you is to create that stillness. Just one minute a day to get quiet and listen. What is it that you are being called to?

If you can't hear right now, don't worry. This book is going to help you listen. It will support you to drop the weight of what's holding you back, help you answer your calling, tap into your potential, and unleash your greatness into the world that needs your message. In the chapters that follow, we'll explore what it truly means to be a purpose-driven influencer, how to regain your authenticity, embrace your uniqueness, and avoid the catastrophic pitfalls of chasing popularity. This journey will empower you to stand secure in your difference, inspire others, and transform lives without being tethered to the ever-distracting loop of dopamine hits from likes. It's time to step into the realm of purpose-driven influence, where your impact is lasting, your energy abundant, and your fulfillment unwavering. This is the path of the purpose-driven influencer, and together, we're embarking on this transformative journey.

So what exactly is a purpose-driven influencer? We'll get deeper into that later in the book but for now... It's simply defined as an individual who commits to taking a heart-led approach to making a positive and

> LIFE IS ALWAYS SPEAKING TO YOU IN TINY WHISPERS INTENDED TO GENTLY MOVE YOU IN THE DIRECTION OF YOUR DESTINY.

meaningful impact in the lives of others. Driven by a higher purpose, they authentically lead and inspire, leveraging their influence to effect positive change, foster personal growth, and contribute to the well-being of individuals and communities.

PART ONE
A Higher Calling

Chapter One

Becoming A Purpose-Driven Influencer

"The two most important days in your life are the day you are born and the day you find out why."
—Mark Twain

Reflecting on my life, I realize that I was raised with the principles of a purpose-driven influencer long before I understood what it meant. Back then, I didn't have a name for it because I was living it without the need to label it. Times have changed, and so has the way we serve the world, but I didn't always recognize the path I was meant to follow.

As a child, I was brought up in a religious household. Every Sunday, my grandmother would take me to church. My mother would ensure I was dressed in a crisp suit, and off I'd go with my grandmother. Once we reached the church, I'd sit beside her on those blue church benches. I was about five years old, too young to understand the sermons, but I observed the congregation's actions. These were my first examples of purpose-driven influencers.

The committed members of the congregation were dedicated to making a difference, living out their belief in "Doing God's work" or "Ministry" as they would call it. Their actions, the way they treated each other, the community outreach, and mission trips to countries like Haiti, left a lasting impression on me. It was beautiful to witness. Everyone had a role to play, and they executed their duties with grace and joy. No one sought fame or recognition, no elaborate titles or lengthy credentials in their bios; they were simply servants. Their driving force was pure purpose, nothing more, nothing less. Many elements contributed to the success of a Sunday service, and I knew it involved a team effort. After the service, I'd observe individuals stacking chairs in a corner, others mopping and cleaning, and some bringing in the food they had prepared the night before to share with the congregation and the pastor. These selfless acts of service deeply inspired me, so much so that I became one of them as I got older. I began helping out by stacking chairs, mopping, and taking care of whatever needed to be done.

Now I understand why my grandmother brought me to church every Sunday. A purposeful upbringing was part of a larger cosmic plan that ultimately prepared me for life as a purpose-driven influencer. I was placed in an environment where purpose-driven work was the norm, where my grandmother instilled in me the importance of serving and giving back. She taught me to let purpose be the guiding force in my life. She'd say; *"Do everything with the right heart, for God, and the universe will bless you. Don't do it for man."* In other words, don't seek recognition and applause from people, because the work you do serves a higher purpose. As the saying goes, *"Man gives you awards, but God gives you the reward."*

There is a reward for purpose-driven influencers who serve the world. Being a purpose-driven influencer is about your heart and intention. Purpose is a driving force that fills you with energy, joy, and fulfillment when you aim to uplift others. But when you're hustling for your worth, and focusing on the wrong objectives, it becomes exhausting. Purpose is supposed to invigorate you, not drain you. It's only tiring when you're chasing validation and doing it for the wrong reasons. The universe is hitting the like button on your actions every time they are in service to humanity and the world. You don't need to be witnessed by others, because the universe is witnessing you all the time. When you're doing good and leading with the right intentions, you'll experience fulfillment like no other.

Social media platforms, especially if you're new to them, can feel like an entirely different world. I remember my initial hesitation about joining these platforms, especially Facebook, which my Aunt Chantel tried to convince me to join countless times. I used to tell her I wanted no part of " Waste-Book" as I used to call it. I just didn't see any point in it, plus I enjoyed living my life in a very low-key manner.

> THE UNIVERSE IS HITTING THE LIKE BUTTON ON YOUR ACTIONS EVERY TIME THEY ARE IN SERVICE TO HUMANITY AND THE WORLD. YOU

When my wife and I first started dating, she embarked on a mission that felt more intense than any FBI background check. Why? Well, it turned out I was a rare species in the modern dating jungle—I had no social media presence whatsoever. As she searched through the virtual landscape, desperately trying to find a Facebook profile or at least a tweet, she couldn't help but raise an eyebrow in suspicion. She thought It was super weird, raising a red flag. *"Why don't you have any social media?"* she inquired, her detective instincts fully activated. I just shrugged, not bothered by the fact that I'm not part of the online sharing club. *"Nothing's wrong; I just don't use social media,"* I told her, keeping it simple. Eventually, she persuaded me to join because she knew I had a passion for motivating people and she thought Instagram would be the perfect place to share my gift for inspiring people.

So, with her belief behind me, I opened an Instagram account to share the motivational quotes I had written. The world of influencers and creatives on social media was bustling, and I felt like the new kid on the block. It was a bit like being in a new school where you didn't know anyone. In my case, I had no followers initially, except for one dedicated supporter who liked everything I posted and thought my content was amazing—my wife. Her encouragement kept me going, and as time went on, more followers trickled in. I started posting daily, sharing what inspired me and what I was learning about life. I was still trying to understand how it all worked, as it was foreign territory to me. As my followers increased, something interesting happened. I realized that many people on these platforms shared similar gifts and talents. While we all knew deep down that we were unique, it was challenging to maintain that belief when we saw so much similarity. I discovered that the gift of motivation I had was also possessed by many others on my platform, but they had more followers than I did. Strangely, those numbers triggered feelings of inadequacy and competition. Judgment kicked in in response to this, and I began to think; *"This person isn't better than me."* I became critical of what others were posting in order to deal with the feelings of inadequacy that this social media world had created within me. Instead of addressing these negative feelings and my own behavior, I carried on as if this were the norm. I continued posting daily, even sharing content that didn't resonate with me. I started to lose sight of who I truly was. The pressure to keep up with other influencers led me to believe that I needed to post as frequently as they did.

The influencers I followed were posting up to five times a day, and I quickly learned that if I had any hope of becoming successful, that's what was required of me. I hungrily consumed the content of every social media expert I could find, all of them imploring me to post as often as possible to even have a hope of getting seen amongst the cut-throat and ever-changing algorithms. But it wasn't just about volume, it was also about timing. I had to learn a formula; the right content, with the right imagery, at the right time, and the right frequency. It was a daunting, enormous task, but I felt the pressure to meet this benchmark, it felt like the only way to remain relevant and inspirational. There was a lot at stake and a lot to get wrong. As stress flooded my body, my creativity began to wane. I would feel pressure to post followed by euphoria when that post received a like or comment. This daily dance of doom severed my connection to my original purpose. Just like that, any intention or authenticity behind what I was posting got replaced by an obsession with the numbers. With each check off of my daily social media to-do list, I veered further away from the values I held as a child going to church with my grandmother. I was no longer the person who saw purpose in serving; I had become someone else.

Gradually, I grew exhausted, not from creating content that inspired my followers but from trying to keep up with what everyone else was doing. Purpose should energize you, not exhaust you, but the energy I spent was on the wrong pursuits. Purpose should bring you joy and vitality. I was tired of hustling for my worth. If I didn't receive many likes on a post, I interpreted it as a reflection of my worth and the quality of my work. The number of likes dictated my happiness and my self-esteem. The more likes and comments I received, the happier I became, and the opposite occurred when the likes were few. It felt like a caffeine crash combined with a blow to my self-esteem.

Perhaps you've come across a meme that humorously captures this behavior, and I'm sure you can relate to it. The meme shows someone snorting a rolled-up piece of paper, with the substance being "likes." Likes have become the new social media drug for many users. Research has shown that receiving a like on your social media content triggers the release of dopamine, a pleasure-associated hormone in your brain. It's like taking a drug, and the cycle can become addictive. I've never experimented with drugs, but I do understand that the highs can lead to lows, and addicts are constantly searching for their next high. The same applies to social media users who chase the next hit of dopamine in the form of likes. Experts, including those featured in the eye-opening documentary, "The Social Dilemma", available to watch on Netflix at the time of publication, caution about how social media platforms are designed to keep you hooked. Notifications, algorithms, and the constant flow of content are intentionally crafted to grab and keep our attention. They want you to spend as much time as possible on the platform because that is what makes their platform successful. Therefore, their algorithms are designed in a way that will meet their goals. This is what makes social media addictive and we are seeing rising proof that it is negatively impacting the well-being of millions. In a 2020 New York Times article, Anna Lembke, an addiction expert at Stanford University, said that social media companies *"exploit the brain's evolutionary need for interpersonal connection."* Experts encourage us to be mindful and strike a balance when using these platforms. So, as you navigate the digital realm, remember to stay true to your path while making a positive impact online.

I've experienced the highs, the likes I eagerly sought, and the positive feedback from followers who were inspired by my content, but even with these successes, I knew something was off. Something deeper was happening within me that needed to be addressed and corrected. I had to break free from this unhealthy cycle.

If you're anything like me, you might have reached a point in your influencer journey where you're weary. You're tired of posting without a clear purpose, tired of the competitive race for likes, tired of the addiction to dopamine-driven engagement. You want to be authentic with your message and make a genuine difference without feeling threatened by the influencers around you. As a purpose-driven influencer, you can evolve to a level of self-worth that means a single like, just one solitary person telling you that you've changed their life, would mean more to you than a million people saying it. You can break free from the exhausting pursuit of your worth and find genuine purpose.

There's a title for those who yearn for such freedom and fulfillment. It's a title I've embraced as my new identity, and it's one I invite you to adopt as well. The destiny you're meant to fulfill requires something greater than the fleeting satisfaction social media can provide. You deserve something greater, a deeper sense of purpose that doesn't wane after your first like on a post. You need a higher purpose, a loftier ambition, and a greater calling in your life. I invite you to become a purpose-driven influencer. I invite you to declare it now.

Take Action:

Stand up, put your hand over your heart, and say aloud; "*I am a purpose-driven influencer and I am committed to doing good in the world*".

Chapter Two

It's Not About You

"Once you can live from the foundation of knowing your life is about the lives you touch, you'll finally be able to step into the life you've longed to live, awakened to the Divine expression of who you truly are."

—Neale Donald Walsch

A few short years ago, life looked very different. I was depressed. Everything I thought I understood about life was being called into question; God, the universe, my life path, and what I was supposed to be doing with my time on Earth. I was finding it hard to connect back to that teenage boy overcoming his fears and inspiring an entire congregation, I was lost. Stuck in a pity party that no one would RSVP to. Not even God Himself, or so I'd told myself, because, of course, He was attempting to get through to me. One morning, He finally succeeded...

I had woken up immediately gripped by the funk that had become my norm. I lay in bed and said; *"I want to be happy, I want to be happy, I want to be happy."*

As I spoke these words out loud, it was as if someone was eavesdropping on a personal conversation I was having with myself. I began to hear an echo of my words, but the word that had the loudest echo was *"I"*. It was vibrating, loud and sharp, as though someone was screaming my words back to me over an intercom. Slowly, as I listened in shock, a new voice emerged, a softer, whispering voice. It said;

"As long as the focus of your life is about you, you will never be happy or live in the fullness of your purpose." It hit me like a punch to the chest. I had been guided back to my inner voice of truth and in that one moment, I realized my depression was nothing more than a symptom of veering from purpose. It was the result of a lapse in concentration that allowed my ego to take over and run the show. The ego is the part of us that is constantly absorbed with self. It has to be, its purpose is to keep our physical body safe, but if you want a purpose-driven life, it can't be the one in charge. In *"The Seven Spiritual Laws of Success"*[1] Deepak Chopra says, *"The question of what's in it for me, is the internal dialogue of the ego. Asking "How can I help" is the internal dialogue of the spirit. The spirit is the domain of your awareness where you experience your universality. "In just shifting your internal dialogue from "What's in it for me?" to "How can I help?" you automatically go beyond the ego into the domain of your spirit".*

If you want to be a purpose-driven influencer, you have to change your dialogue and make it one about your contribution to the world around you. Serving is the language of the universe.

That experience shook me and awakened me to the reality that I was preoccupied with myself. All I could think about was me, my needs, my life's purpose, my calling, my work, my this, and my that. Just a bunch of ME, ME, ME!!

> AS LONG AS THE FOCUS OF YOUR LIFE IS ABOUT YOU, YOU WILL NEVER BE HAPPY OR LIVE IN THE FULLNESS OF YOUR PURPOSE.

If you are going to live the type of life that touches people with your social platforms, and your daily life, you have to remove the focus of your life off of yourself and place it on others. It's not easy, but outward living is where purpose thrives. Whenever you feel like you are lost, or as if your life has no value, I can almost guarantee you are caught up with yourself. You're too focused on what is not going right, or how many followers liked your post, or trying to get people to follow you, and criticizing yourself and comparing yourself with the next influencer. You're in your head, which keeps you disconnected from your heart. Now, whenever I find myself questioning or doubting, I shift my mind to service. Gandhi observed, *"that the best way to find yourself is to lose yourself in the service of others."* It's in the service of others that you find clarity of purpose. In the moments of doubt and confusion that you will encounter when you feel lost and as if life has no meaning, I want you to shift to a service mindset.

Here is how I move into a "service state of mind", you are welcome to emulate this list, but I encourage you to create your own:

- Call someone

- Send an encouraging text

- Say a prayer for someone

- Write a letter

- Smile at a stranger

As the saying goes, "When you feel helpless, help someone."

Success Is The Result of Prioritizing Value

For a long time, I procrastinated on writing this book. As well as the natural doubts that tend to plague the mind when a new challenge presents itself, I was worried it would distract from growing my social media and reaching more people. It took conscious effort to say yes to this challenge, and a willingness to keep committing to service every single day. I believe when something is supposed to be delivered to the world through you, it will keep asking for a limited time, if you ignore it for long enough, it will find someone else who will take the action necessary to get it out into the world. Don't be surprised if the ideas you've refused to bring to life manifest in the world through someone else's hands. As motivational speaker, Les Brown, says; *"The graveyard is the richest place on earth because it is here that you will find all the hopes and dreams that were never fulfilled, the books that were never written, the songs that were never sung, the inventions that were never shared, the cures that were never discovered, all because someone was too afraid to take that first step..."* You are simply a vessel, you can answer the call or not. I felt so passionate about this message, the thought of it being delivered through someone else and the knowledge that I had said no to such an important assignment is something I couldn't tolerate, and so I got to work. If you don't chase your dreams, the regret of not pursuing them will always be chasing you. A lot of people, perhaps yourself included, are sitting on ideas, talent, and visions, and are too scared to act.

People procrastinate for years, and yet I know if they saw their ideas in the world, manifested through someone else, that would crush them. As my mother-in-law has said to me many times; *"God would rather change the person than change the plan. If there is a divine assignment for you to do, you have to surrender and answer the call - you do not want a substitute".* I had to choose between what I thought would bring me more success in the short term, and what was ultimately going to be of the highest value to society. My social media will always be there, but this book wouldn't be.

> IF YOU DON'T CHASE YOUR DREAMS, THE REGRET OF NOT PURSUING THEM WILL ALWAYS BE CHASING YOU.

There is a reason why, as influencers, you can easily get distracted from your calling. The number one thing you are going to be at war with daily is reminding yourself that the purpose of your platform, your creative domain, and most of all your life – is bigger than you. We are all wired with the need to succeed and a desire to put a dent in the universe, but the only way to be of service to the people who follow you is by focusing on your assignment and what you show up to give back to the world. When you decide that you are going to use your gifts and talents as an offering to genuinely impact other people's lives instead of trying to use them for simply just material gain or to satisfy an ego desire, success is going to follow. One thing we should all keep in mind as we strive for more influence in the world is to remember that the goal is to not only be successful, but we should also aim to be valuable. I believe when we take this approach to our influence, we are going to attract success because our ambition is fueled by the desire to serve.

We all want our lives to matter. It's the reason we do the things we do. We pursue influence because we want to make a difference. There's nothing wrong with the pursuit of influence, but I want you to know this quest alone won't change the world. What is going to change the world is when your influence leaves people better than you found them.

Influence is about serving and leading others to change. Let's face it, we live in an age where everyone is calling themselves an influencer or digital creator and that is something that is not going to change. Every day, a new influencer is born, someone starts a social media account and gives themselves the title of influencer without considering or even knowing the responsibility that comes with that title. But what are you really influencing?

Motivational speaker, Prince EA, gave an amazing speech you can find on Instagram or YouTube about influencers that really speaks to the point I'm trying to make here. This is what he said:

> WHAT IS GOING TO CHANGE THE WORLD IS WHEN YOUR INFLUENCE LEAVES PEOPLE BETTER THAN YOU FOUND THEM.

"That word influencer is interesting to me because it's like, we're influencing people to do what? A lot of people call themselves social media influencers, but you're influencing people to do what? Is it to reach a level of beauty? That is not attainable naturally? Is it to have people lust after cars? Or material objects that will never bring

somebody true happiness? Is this what it means to be an influencer? You know, when you get pulled over, you're drunk. They say you're under the influence. A lot of people are intoxicated by what these influencers put out there. When you get sick, what do they say? You've come down with influenza. A lot of people are ill... because of what these influencers put out there. So I just have one question... for every influencer... Because we're all influencers, and that question is, when people come to your page: Do they walk away better or worse?"

Cue in the slow clap for this speech. I wish I had been in this room when he was delivering it because I would have been the person clapping and cheering the loudest. This is a guy who gets it, he has a purpose-driven influencer mindset. After visiting your page, or simply being in your presence do people walk away better or worse? Take a second, and think about this question. As a matter of fact, go to your social media right now and look at the last couple of things you posted. Take a moment and do a quick audit of your content right now. Imagine you are the person seeking inspiration, or some sort of guidance. Does your content provide that? Does it inspire you to be better or did it leave you feeling worse? Let the answer to this question be the catalyst to inspire you to keep building on the good you've been putting out into the universe, or move you to make a spiritual, and service-based pivot.

You have to constantly be aware of how you are flowing in your influence so you do not lose sight of what your assignment is. Every day you have to measure the quality and impact of your influence by what you post, how you treat people, the words you speak, your contribution to the world, and how you nourish the relationships in your life. In other words, you have to keep yourself on purpose by examining your life, because it easily gets off track. At the end of each day, I encourage you to take a moment and pause and reflect on how you used your influence. The results should either applaud you or correct you. People will know you by what you share, and what you share determines what kind of influencer you are. The fruit of your influence is who people become. If your life inspires others to dream more, do more, and become more, you are a purpose-driven influencer. If your content and the way you show up for your audience are helping them to become happier, more peaceful, kinder, and more successful people, you are chasing value instead of success, and you are a purpose-driven influencer.

Mops & Buckets - Secrets From A Millionaire

When I was 23 years old, I worked at the YMCA as a fitness attendant. During one of my shifts, I recall having a conversation with a millionaire. He was in his sixties and I was so intrigued by how he had become successful and wealthy, I was desperate to pick his brain. I eagerly asked him what his secret was. My ears were ready; my eyes were locked in on this man as I was waiting for him to share the most sage advice on how to make it big.

"You want to be successful and rich?" he said.

I said yes with a big smile, and he replied;

"Mops and buckets kid, mops and buckets."

Mops and buckets, really? I pressed him a little more for a better answer, thinking he would say something different, but he repeated in his rugged voice;

"Mops and buckets kid, mops and buckets."

He must be kidding me, right? How are mops and buckets going to help me become successful in life? But he was right, mops and buckets are the way. For me, quite literally. At the time, I wanted to be in the hospitality industry badly, so I called a hotel in New Jersey asking if they were hiring. They said yes, and to my surprise, they asked if I could come in for an interview the same day. It went so great that they hired me on the spot and asked me to start the same week. I was hired as an overnight houseman, but I had my sights on becoming an executive someday. My duties were cleaning the bathrooms of the hotel lobby, making sure the exterior of the hotel was clean, and last but not least, mopping the floors!! Honestly, I was excited to get a foot in the door, and if it meant holding a mop and bucket, I would be the best cleaner that place has ever seen. All I could hear as I mopped the lobby floor was that elusive old millionaire chuckling; *"Mops and buckets kid, mops and buckets."* I did my job with excellence, I did it with a smile, and I did it with gratitude, hoping I would one day get noticed and begin my climb to the top. But, as an overnight cleaner, nobody sees you. All the executives, the general manager, and most of the staff are usually in by 9 am and gone by 7 pm. I wasn't sure how my goals would ever manifest, but I kept my focus on being as valuable as I possibly could. Six months into the job, they got rid of my position, but the company didn't want to get rid of me. Instead, they hired me to be the host for the restaurant. I went from not being seen on the overnight shift to working during the day. Finally, management could witness my skill set for serving on display and how I served guests with passion and purpose. As time went on, I became one of the best employees at the company.

Within 2 years, I achieved my goal of becoming an executive for that hotel.

The universe is always conspiring to promote you when you serve to the best of your ability and provide consistent, selfless value to those who are seeking it. I don't care what job you have, if you show up with the right attitude and do it with excellence, good things will begin to happen for you. The same is true for your path to becoming a great social media influencer. I don't care if you don't have a big platform to begin with, that shouldn't be your focus. Simply view every opportunity as a way to serve and create impact, and the following will come. Your influence is only as big as your perspective. Martin Luther King Jr said it best; *"If a man is called to be a street sweeper, he should sweep streets even as Michelangelo painted, or Beethoven composed music, or Shakespeare wrote poetry. He should sweep streets so well that all the hosts of Heaven and Earth will pause to say, here lived a great street sweeper who did his job well."*

Show up each day prepared to offer value, and people will notice. Excellence is always remembered. This is what the scripture means when it says, *"A man's gift makes room for him and brings him before the great."* - Proverbs 18:16. God has put a gift or talent in every person that the world will make room for. Your gift is the mop and the world is the bucket, create a flawless relationship between the two, and it is this gift that will enable you to be influential.

Define Your Own Success & Stay True To It

Vince Lomarbdi said; *'The man on top of the mountain didn't fall there"*. Influence requires that you make peace with the fact that you are going to have to climb. You are going to have to commit to the process of becoming the influencer you envision yourself being even if you don't see the results. That is what you call holding the vision and trusting the process. Right now, in our social media craze culture, there is a race going on to be a top influencer, a race to succeed, and to be the best. Getting caught up in this race is where a lot of influencers fail. Instead of focusing on their own vision and purpose, they succumb to joining the multitude of influencers who don't have a service mentality. I have seen so many trade in the authenticity of their mission in an attempt to fast-track their elevation. When it seems as though everyone is advancing faster than you, it can be very easy to start to run toward someone else's definition of success and, without realizing it, abandon your own vision for your life. When we get caught up in the race for success, we start to try and be like everyone else instead of being patient and working on the things that really make us come alive. But being a copycat will only ever give the illusion of success, even if you amassed a huge following and became wealthy, you would not be fulfilled, because you've attained it under the pretenses of an inauthentic projection of yourself. If you want true success, you have to block out what everyone else is doing, and just keep climbing your own mountain. I like what Condoleezza Rice said; *"People who end up as 'first' don't actually set out to be first. They set out to do something they love."* Purpose-driven influencers focus on passion, they keep their focus on the love of the work. If you focus on the work, the work will take care of everything else. Results before recognition. As Arlan Hamilton said, *"Be yourself so that the people looking for you can find you."*

You Can't Rush Greatness

Anyone who knows New York City will be familiar with the snail's pace of the trains running local after certain hours. As they slowly make every single stop, what could be a quick commute home ends up becoming a long, laborious journey. I used to get so frustrated when riding the local train, but I could do nothing to speed up my commute. I had two choices; be upset about it or enjoy the ride home. So I decided to transform my frustration into inspiration. I used that time to be productive. I would read, journal, or plan for the next day, and see it as a growth opportunity. Just like those New York City trains, life will go through different seasons and schedules. There will be times when it is moving very quickly and everything seems to be happening all at once, and there will be times when it is making every single stop, forcing you to be more aware of your surroundings and asking you to match this slower pace. One of the issues with social media is it perpetuates the idea that we should be in a certain place in our lives at a certain time. You may have said things like; *"I am thirty years old and I'm still not married"*, or, *"I should be more successful by now"*, or, *"I should have a bigger platform already, this person has millions of followers, that's what I should have"*. If you take one thing from this book, let it be this... Your influence is not an express train. It's been said that *"slow success builds character. Fast success builds the ego."* The influence train is always running locally. You can't fast-track your destiny. You are going to be very miserable in your pursuit of greatness if you are expecting success to happen fast. You might as well sit back and enjoy the slow ride of becoming the influencer you were born to be. The most important thing on the influencer journey is not speed, it's progress. The culture of instant gratification that has been born as a result of the technological age has conditioned us to believe that we should expect things at the snap of a finger. It's this mindset that has created a lot of frustrated influencers. This attitude has held me back and kept me frustrated with my path to influence, and it will do the same for you if you don't learn to recognize it and reframe it. Your desired timeline may well be different from your destined timeline. But if you're constantly chasing overnight success, you'll become discouraged, possibly to the point where you stop going after your dreams altogether. When it comes to influence, speed is your enemy, patience is your friend.

No Matter What, Just Start!

I believe the reason so many people don't share their gifts or don't have the courage to begin their influencer journey is that the perception of starting at the bottom robs them of their influencer potential. As Mark Twain once said; *"The secret to getting ahead is getting started."* As you begin the journey, you will find every excuse not to start. You will come up with all the reasons why you are not ready, and why it's not time yet. You don't need to have it all figured out yet to be an influencer, you just need to begin. You have to trust that you will be guided as you start taking the steps. This is where we have to remember what Joseph Cambell told us; *"we must follow our bliss"*. There is an inner calling within everyone that beckons us to come forward to be the heroes in our own stories.

Fall In Love With The Process

Becoming an influencer is about who you get to become, not about what you can get. It's easy to get so goal-driven that you forget to enjoy the journey. Athletes are well known for saying that the secret to greatness is to fall in love with the process. Why? Because if you fall in love with the process, you are going to love what the process produces. There is no better place to learn who you are than right inside the process. It is the training ground, it is the influencer's gym where you train your stamina daily so you can be in this for the long haul. In the same way that going to the gym once, or occasionally, won't get you the results you desire, you won't master your influence in one day, or one year. It's going to take a lifetime of commitment, discipline, and consistency of effort to show up day in, and day out. Even on the days when you don't feel like it. It has been said that *"commitment is doing the thing you said you were going to do long after the mood you had said it in has left you"*. For years, I would start things, and if I didn't see immediate results, I would get frustrated with my progress and quit. Immediate gratification is the number one killer of purpose and influence.

It makes you believe that if you are not producing and growing quickly, then whatever your form of creative expression is not what you are suited for. That is a lie. Your influence is a seed, and the day you plant the seed is not the day you see the result. You have to nurture it, and just because you don't see any growth doesn't mean that growth is not happening. I remember learning how to play the bass guitar, a friend of mine had already been learning for a couple of months and their progress inspired me. But I quickly fell into the trap of measuring my progress against theirs. This, of course, discouraged me because I was never going to measure up to someone who had more experience than me and was further along the path than I was. But I allowed my self-judgment to influence me to quit. Do not forget that whilst you influence others, you are also influencing yourself. Mastery of your passions takes time. Honing your craft takes time. If you are looking around you and measuring your influence against others, I want you to stop that right now because that is not serving you. It's going to make you quit before you even give yourself a chance to see your abilities fully develop into something great. If you work at your gift, your gift will end up working for you. Keep going!

Here are 3 key Principles to apply to help grow your Influence:

1. Patience and Persistence: Think of your influence as a seed. Just as a farmer nurtures the soil, you have to keep nurturing the soil of your influence, even when there is

no sign of growth. When you haven't gained any new followers, or there are no new subscribers in sight, or no comments on the post you worked so hard on, you have trust in the process that you are going to reap a harvest of influence, as long as you do not give up.

2. Unwavering Faith: Purpose-driven Influencers must maintain unwavering faith in their mission and message. Every day you have to feed your faith and starve the doubts in your head. You do this by listening to or reading positive and uplifting messages that are going to help create a coding around your mind that shields you from the negativity that wants to get you off the path of your purpose.

3. Expect Blessings And Breakthroughs: The law of sowing and reaping is undefeated. As you make daily deposits into developing your vision the blessings and breakthroughs will manifest themselves. Patience and persistence plus unwavering faith produce blessings and breakthroughs. Learn to expect them whilst committing to your true vision and they will surely come.

The Gift of Resistance

For years my dream was to become an author, so at the height of the 2020 Covid pandemic, I decided to take steps to make that dream a reality. I partnered with a publishing company that would publish my book, they even set me up with people who were on this same journey as an accountability group. One of the first things I had to do was create an "I am an author" video and upload it to the Facebook group. It was terrifying and liberating at the same time. This was the first time I told the world what I wanted to accomplish. There is power in speaking your dream out loud. But as I started working on the book, life got in the way. My wife and I had a baby which led to me taking a year out to be present with her and our new son. Doubts crept in slowly and I became plagued with thoughts like; *"Am I really a writer?", "Who will want to read my book?"* This is what's known as resistance, and it was kicking my butt. It beat me down so bad that soon enough I just stopped working on the book. I lost all my momentum and my belief in myself. But if there is just one thing I have become absolutely certain of on this journey, when there is a true calling in your life, that calling will keep calling until you answer. Steven Pressfield states; *"The more important a call to action is to our soul's evolution, the more resistance we will feel about answering it."* Resistance is confirmation of your dreams.

Don't Procrastinate On Your Destiny

As creators, withholding the valuable contributions we're meant to share with the world is a clear sign that we haven't gotten over ourselves. You might be thinking, 'I'm not ready; I'm not good enough.' However, it's not about you. Get out of the way so you can be a blessing to the people you were made to help. It's essential to put ourselves out there; we never know whose life it might impact. There's a powerful saying: 'Your passion is for you; your purpose is for others.' I discovered that the biggest obstacle to my dreams was me. Taking a real inventory of my life, I confronted the reasons holding me back. Success requires daily habits, not once-in-a-lifetime transformations, as emphasized by author James Clear. On the days filled with motivation, I was unstoppable on my mission. Yet, when faced with doubts or lacked inspiration, I treated my dreams as if they didn't matter. Procrastination is assuming tomorrow is promised. Embracing purpose-driven influence demands commitment and action. Stop procrastinating on your destiny because someone needs what you have. Every day you delay is a missed opportunity to impact lives.

Everything Is For Your Growth

Oprah Winfrey said; *"Your life isn't about a big break. It's about taking one significant life-transforming step at a time. Every fulfilled dream occurred because of dedication to the process."* When you set your mind and heart on following the path to your passion and purpose, it often takes seasons of preparation to become who you are destined to be. This is something that never changes. There is no destination, it's about the constant journey of growth and evolution. That is something people often forget about influence. There will be seasons in your life where it seems like nothing is working. You are swinging, but everything is a strikeout. This is the place where you find yourself confused, feeling like progress is not being made, doubting, questioning, in an identity limbo, angry, frustrated, struggling. Perhaps you are broke or jobless and feeling like the universe is just cruel. This is probably going to be hard to receive, but all those things are necessary for your growth. What you go through, grows you. It's those crucible moments that shape you into an influencer who has real authority. No test, no testimony. No mess, no message. If I had not gone through any adversity in my life, I could not have written this book or inspired others to believe in themselves. I'm not a perfect influencer, I still struggle, but I know I can't give up, you can't give up no matter how challenging things may be right now. At times, life just makes you feel like throwing in the towel and leaving your dreams behind. But it's in those moments that something great and magical is getting ready to unfold. So hang in there my friend, because your breakthrough is going to produce the kind of life that makes it all make sense, and you'll be thankful for every moment that got you there.

Everything in your life is preparing you for a moment that is yet to come. You might be on the bench right now, but you are being prepared to be a starter. You might be mopping floors right now, but soon they will be calling you the CEO. There will always be moments of wondering when the breakthrough is going to come, of wondering when life is really going to start or when your visions will become reality. I want you to acknowledge those moments and affirm to yourself; *"I am on my way to greatness, I trust the timing of my life."* We have to trust that everything is happening for our highest good. You are right where you need to be. It may not feel like it right now, but the dots are going to connect. It has been said that *"life is lived forwards but understood backwards"*. Looking back on my life, I needed all the experiences I've had to mold me, and I still trust the process now. Sometimes it feels messy and uncertain, but I don't have to like it, I just have to trust it.

We're used to seeing overnight successes and assuming that person just got lucky. But nobody ever comes out of nowhere, we just don't

> **EVERYTHING IN YOUR LIFE IS PREPARING YOU FOR A MOMENT THAT IS YET TO COME.**

see the process it took to get there. The work, the years of struggle, the rejection, and the hours they put in to hone their craft. The singer who sells out concerts in large stadiums was once the singer who performed for a handful of people in a tiny room. The person who has a million followers started with one. The successful actress was once a waitress who worked late nights so she could audition during the day. There is a common thread in every successful influencer story. No struggle, no influence.

Take a look at these great influencers in the making who didn't start as great in their careers:

- Michael Jordan, regarded as the best basketball player of all time, was cut from his high school basketball team during his sophomore year. He turned the cut into motivation. It fueled him throughout his entire basketball career. It made him a 6 time NBA champion.

- Oprah Winfrey was told by a Baltimore TV producer that she was unfit for television news. She was later fired from her evening news gig as a reporter. Winfrey eventually became the successful host of The Oprah Winfrey Show, which aired for 25 seasons.

- Steve Jobs was fired from Apple, the company he co-founded. His second act turned out to be bigger and better than the first.

- Walt Disney was fired from one of his first animation jobs at the Kansas City Star newspaper because his editor felt he "lacked imagination and had no good ideas".

- J.K. Rowling was a single mother living on welfare, trying to support her daughter. It took her seven years to write the story of Harry Potter and the Sorcerer's Stone, and when she finished, twelve major publishing houses rejected the book.

- Thomas Edison was told by his teachers he was "too stupid to learn anything".

- Albert Einstein didn't start speaking until he was four, reading until he was seven, and was thought to be mentally handicapped.

The people whom we admire the most and view as successful have all been influencers in the making. Success takes time. They have been rejected, failed, struggled, told they were not good enough but persevered through it all. As you go after your influence, you are going to encounter a lot of difficulties along the way, make up your mind and heart now that you are going to fight for your vision of becoming the influencer you aspire to be. Many people who fail are people who give up right when they are close to succeeding.

Take Action:

Take out your journal and write down the following statement. Then spend some time free-writing on the following questions, this is the moment you become purpose-driven.

"Today, I make a commitment to become the purpose-driven influencer I was created to be by taking the following steps":

1. Ask big questions. How can I serve? Journal on what your unique gifts are and how they can help the people who follow you.

2. What can I do today to provide value to my platform, my community, or my family without looking for anything in return? I choose to always put my purpose before my elevation. I understand that elevation comes to those who prioritize purpose.

3. PWP: Post With Purpose. This is the purpose-driven influencer mantra. Write it on a post, put it on your laptop, put in the bathroom mirror, whatever you do, you must remember this. Before you share, think for a moment, what is the intention and energy you want to put into every post? What is the intention you want to convey when you're speaking or making a presentation? Get clear, then make your move.

Write your vision down, and then out of that vision, you will have a north star from which you create from. Purpose-driven influencers create with intention.

Chapter Three
Build Your Inner Brand

"Success is an inside job." —Unknown

Before we set off on the wrong foot, this chapter is not about marketing, you'll need a different book altogether for that. Throughout the next sections of this journey together, you will come to understand who you are and how you want to present yourself. Your purpose-driven brand is created when you are strong and grounded in your own identity, this is what will be palpable from the moment someone lays eyes on you for the first time, either in real life or on your social media pages. You must do the inner work, and the healing, and commit to continual conscious evolution to successfully build your inner brand. This is how you will become instantly recognizable to those who resonate with your message.

We live in a world of selfies and perfectly curated social media feeds that give the illusion of success, but we have no idea what's going on behind the profile. We don't really know the people we follow. We don't know what kind of character they have or if there is congruence between who they are offline with what they share online. Not everyone is what they "post to be". We assume someone is successful based on what they portray online. The influencer world runs entirely on perception. We see the beautiful trips, the glitz and the glam, the cars, the beautiful couple who are #goals, and we are quick to label that as a success. I have fallen guilty of that myself. I've allowed amazing photography and well-written captions or the number of likes to be the qualifier of what success is. But never forget, success is not an external projection, it is an inside job. Never judge success based on what you see outwardly, because nobody can upload the condition of the soul.

It's wrong to judge only on outward appearance because in a way it's only one side of the story. Outward appearance and behavior don't show what is driving and motivating the person on the inside. Outwardly a person can show a great life, but behind closed doors, they may hate the life they have. Outwardly a person can be doing nice things, but inwardly the motives are wrong. Outwardly there are couples in the world constantly posting how happy they are, but inwardly they are disconnected and on the verge of a breakup. Outwardly someone may get millions of likes, but inwardly they don't like themselves. Outwardly they are rich, but on the inside, they are craving something more fulfilling.

A New Way Of Branding

> *"Finding and living in alignment with your inner purpose is the foundation for fulfilling your outer purpose. It is the basis for true success".*
>
> —Eckhart Tolle

I am not a brand expert and if you are looking for advice on how to build a brand from a marketing perspective, you won't get it from this book. What you will get is the wisdom required to heal, to come into alignment with your true self, and to make the commitment to consistently do the inner work that will create the most important aspect of branding there is; YOU. As an influencer, you are building a personal brand, but I want you to think about branding as the presentation of your character, and the authenticity of your nature, rather than something marketable. Trust me, the magnetism of authenticity is the best marketing tool there is!

Marketing experts will tell you that to have a successful brand, you need things like a brand strategy, knowledge of your audience, a logo, and a social media strategy. I'm not saying these things aren't important, but that stuff means nothing without a solid connection to who you are and why you're doing what you're doing. Before we can build a brand on the outside that looks great to the public, we have to build the brand on the inside.

Our culture is obsessed more than ever with image and appearance. Technology and social media cater to the fixation of all things external. Nowadays, there is an app and a filter for everything. If you don't like your body, you can alter it with one click. You can have six-pack abs and muscles in seconds. From time to time, I'll watch a makeup tutorial with my wife, and sometimes I can't believe the transformation. The person is almost unrecognizable. I am all for taking care of yourself, but I believe the purpose of makeup is simply to enhance the beauty that you already have, not to turn you into someone else. People will go broke spending money they don't have to try to be someone they're not. It's the reason cosmetic surgery is such a lucrative business. Everyone is trying to attain perfection, but they never will, it's an illusion. To build your inner brand means to take an inside-out approach to your influence. You have to begin with your character, your intentions, and your soul, so you can be your most authentic self in your life's work. Don't put your brand before your character, put your character before your brand. I believe if we make sure we have the internal congruence, the right spirit, and character, the success we are building on the interior will lead to external rewards. Stephen Covey said; *"Private victories precede public victories."*

As a kid, the focus on my outer appearance started very early. One of my grandmother's traditions was to buy me a new suit every Easter. My mother was the same way, she would dress me up every Sunday to send me off to church. I have to admit, I was indeed the sharpest-looking little gentleman in the church. Even now, as an adult, whenever I call my mother to have conversations about my plans to go somewhere, the first thing that comes out of her mouth is, *"Make sure you look good"*, and my response is always, *"Yes, mom I will look good."*

But sometimes, I'll mess with her by telling her I am dressing down for an event that requires formal attire. I get a good kick out of it every time. As I got older, I learned that it's not what you look like that makes you. It's not what you drive, or how much money you have, it's about who you are as a person that matters. The external brand doesn't make you a purpose-driven influencer, it's the inner brand that awards you this important title. No matter what you're doing externally, you want to build a life that not only looks good on the outside but feels good on the inside.

> NO MATTER WHAT YOU'RE DOING EXTERNALLY, YOU WANT TO BUILD A LIFE THAT NOT ONLY LOOKS GOOD ON THE OUTSIDE BUT FEELS GOOD ON THE INSIDE.

Outer brand vs. inner brand

- Outer brand focuses on attention, the inner brand focuses on intention.

- Outer brand focuses on reputation, inner brand focuses on character.

- Outer brand focuses on making money, inner brand focuses on soul wealth.

- Outer brand focuses on success, inner brand focuses on significance.

- Inner brand MUST come before outer brand if you want to be something that creates a sustainable impact, for yourself and the people you influence.

There Is Only One You

CS Lewis said; *"integrity is doing the right thing, even when no one is watching."* Integrity stems from the Latin word; 'integer', which means whole and complete. When you are a Whole Influencer, there is only ONE you. When you are whole and consistent in character, you are the same influencer off social media as you are on it. You don't even need social media to influence because you bring that same "you" wherever you are, regardless of the circumstance. You don't leave parts of yourself behind. You don't compartmentalize who you are. You don't have a 'work you,' a 'family you,' and a 'social you.' You are YOU, all the time. Alignment is when your online presence matches your offline presence. It's not good enough to only spread the good vibes online, you need to BE the good vibes wherever you go. Who are you when nobody is watching? Who are you when you are not posting content? Are you the person who embodies the positivity that you post in real life? Or are you just "Doing it for the gram"? True influencers are more than messengers, they *are* the message they want to deliver. The rule for authentic influence is this: Whatever you want people to become, you must become it first. You have to model what you want others to be. You can't be an authority without authenticity. People can tell when you are not being sincere and honest, they can detect that. I recall someone left a comment on one of my posts that said; *"I love your energy."* How can someone love my energy when they've never physically met me? Because intentions and energy will always shine through.

If you want to connect with your audience and you want to be a leader worth following, you must start with authenticity. There are a lot of influencers who appear to have authority, but they lack authenticity. The world is filled with pseudo-influencers and the way to create separation is to be fully you with no substitutions or illusions. Authority is more than having a large following, an eye-catching bio, or a nice title, you need to be the embodiment of what you are putting out in the universe. Everything you do in real life, everything you do in your job, and in your relationships must always have a piece of you in the message, if it doesn't, it's just hollow words for show.

Three Ways To Create Authentic Power And Influence

1. Embrace Your Uniqueness: Authenticity begins when you decide to lean into your uniqueness. Your greatest asset and superpower lies in your individuality. You have a special influencer DNA that separates you from everyone else. You don't have to post like them, talk like them, or be like them, you can be you and that alone is enough. Do not conform to the influencer world but be the light that

transforms the influencer world by your authentic power. Your Audience will connect with you more deeply when they see the unfiltered version of you. Bring that version of you to whatever and wherever you create.

2. Transparency Transforms: Share your losses as much as you share your wins. I can't trust an influencer who doesn't share the struggle of what it took for them to become who they are now. Pull back the curtains and show your audience the steps you took. Bring us on the journey of growth with you. It's why I enjoy the Instagram vs reality post. It is a reminder nobody's life is perfect no matter how it may seem. At times we only see the end result but not the many failed attempts to get that one piece of content right. We see the end result of success but not many show the process it took to get there. This will help your followers connect with you on a human level. You transform others through transparency.

3. Let Your Values Drive Your Purpose: To Build your inner brand authentically, align your actions and content with your core values. Service and Purpose are the core values that drive my life so everything I do flows from these values. When you are a Purpose Driven Influencer, you understand that purpose dictates your decision-making and what you choose to put out in this world. Identify the values that mean the most to you and let them guide your purpose. Integrate your values into your influencer persona and create from that place.

Empty Words Lead To Empty Influence

Influence minus character equals entertainment. You might as well be a well-trained actor. Lights, camera, action! You are just putting on a show. The scripture puts it this way, in the passage 1 Corinthians 1:13; *"If I speak with human eloquence and angelic ecstasy but don't love, I'm nothing but the creaking of a rusty gate"* That is so powerful! Without love and integrity fueling your influence, you are simply a noise maker. You can look like an influencer on the outside, having thousands of followers, a verified profile, and a great bio, but if the love and intention are not there, you have no lasting power.

I've been blessed to meet some amazing influencers in my life, some have become mentors due to my day job. I work for one of the most popular luxury hotels in Manhattan, New York in guest services. From Oscar-winning actors, athletes, musicians, and reality stars, I've seen them all and have served them all. The thing I am most fascinated by when a big VIP is coming to the hotel is not what they are wearing, it's not the possibility of taking a picture so I can post on social media or brag to my friends, it's what kind of person they are in real life. I want to know if the TV persona is just that, a persona. I want to know if they are kind people. I want to know if they will say thank you, if they will tip our housekeepers, concierge, and runners who will go the distance to purchase whatever they need from the store to make their stay enjoyable. I want to know if they are a representation of the quote; *"You treat the janitor with the same respect you treat the CEO."* These are the things I am always curious about. I am not impressed by money, social status, job title, or the amount of followers a person may have, I'm impressed by the way someone treats other human beings. Like Dwayne Johnson said, *"It's nice to be important, but it's more important to be nice"*

I have had my fair share of disappointment with a lot of people I've met. I know we're not all perfect, and we all have off days, so I am always willing to give people the benefit of the doubt and grace because I need it myself. However, when you are consistent in not being kind, it is no longer an off day, it's just who you are. Our hotel often brings influencers in to stay and promote the hotel on their social media feeds as a way to attract more customers. What a cool gig! You get to stay for free, get to try some of the chef's favorite dishes, and then you upload your experience to Instagram. The fun part is, I get to play a role in this experience. I also got a cool gig. One day, I had the pleasure of meeting the influencer from hell. This lady was nasty. She was mean and downright disrespectful. She was making all sorts of demands, asking me for complementary things that I was not willing to give her. After politely rejecting her demands, she said to me; *"Do you know who I am?"* She then proceeded to tell me she was an influencer, she had thousands of followers on social media and she was trying out our hotel to see if it was worth recommending to her followers. She mentioned she had the power to bring in a lot of revenue to the place. I could not believe this lady was acting the way she did. After our contentious interaction ended, I decided I would do a little research on this "influencer". I found her Instagram page, and yes she was right,

> INFLUENCE MINUS CHARACTER EQUALS ENTERTAINMENT.

she had thousands of followers and she was verified. She had all the external appearances of an influencer. However, the lady in person was totally different from the person I was looking at on Instagram. I browsed her entire page, everything she posted was about positivity. But wait for the kicker, I found one post where she was staying at a different hotel, and in the picture, she was holding a five-dollar bill. She spoke about tipping and making sure you treat hotel workers nicely because they are really hard-working people. Well in my experience, she was the total opposite of all her posts. Let this be a lesson, you need to continually check if your influence on others is trending positive or negative.

Social media is an illusion more often than not. You should see it as no more than a tool for reaching more people than you could offline, but your greatest priority should be who and how you are offline. I believe that our greatest influence begins offline. Sometimes we get caught up influencing people that we cannot even touch and we miss out on the people that are within our reach. You are influencing all the time, if you can't get it right in real life, you have no business taking yourself out to the masses with social media. Start with real life, be intentional and purposeful with every single interaction you have.

> I BELIEVE THAT OUR GREATEST INFLUENCE BEGINS OFFLINE. SOMETIMES WE GET CAUGHT UP INFLUENCING PEOPLE THAT WE CANNOT EVEN TOUCH AND WE MISS OUT ON THE PEOPLE THAT ARE WITHIN OUR REACH.

Stay Humble So You Don't Mishandle Your Success

You may well remember how the actor Will Smith behaved at the 2022 Oscars, it dominated the headlines. On one of the biggest nights of his career, he slapped comedian, Chris Rock, across the face live on TV in response to a joke made about his wife, Jada Pinkett-Smith. I remember thinking it must have been part of a skit, but as I watched Smith heading back to his seat, you could tell this had not been scripted. Later in the show, as he accepted his Best Actor award for his role in the film, King Richard, you could tell the incident had ruined his big moment. In his speech, he shared something Denzel Washington had said to him shortly after the infamous slap; *"At your highest moment, be careful, that's when the devil comes for you"*. At a career-defining moment, Will Smith let his unhealed inner parts dictate how he presented himself. For months, his brand became; "person who lashes out at the slightest offense". This is why working on your inner brand is so critical because if you don't deal with the stuff that is going on within you in private, it will sabotage you in your highest moment. There is a piece of advice that has always stuck with me; *"if you don't deal with your traumas, your traumas will deal with you."*

Without a doubt, success and influence bring with them great rewards, but they also come with a greater opportunity for failure. Some of the greatest leaders, athletes, celebrities, and presidents of our time have fallen due to the mishandling of success. As someone once told me; *"Your gifts and talents will take you places where your character can't keep you".* It's something that we should all keep in mind as we pursue greater influence in the world. The higher you go in life, the more you are going to experience things that are going to try to bring you down. You will face attacks, temptations, distractions, opposition, criticism, and everything in between. The greater the influence the deeper the humility needs to be.

You Can Not Be Purpose-Driven Without A Commitment To Healing

I don't think we can master our inner brand without addressing the parts of us that need to be healed. The purpose of healing is so you can become fully you, without the negative projections of any pain and trauma you have experienced. The hardships you have been through in life can and should shape your purpose and influence, but you must heal first so you can hold them in neutrality and lead from the lessons they provided you with. You have to feel it to heal it. When you integrate the experience into yourself and become whole again, this will impact your contribution to the world. When you neglect the inner work of healing your trauma, emotional health, and mindset, you limit your greatness, and you open yourself up to a cycle of self-sabotage. Avoiding the healing work will ultimately disconnect you from your creative self. By committing to the inner work, you have an opportunity to progress in your soul toward even greater wholeness. I look at the importance of doing the inner work like this: Imagine your creative ideas, visions, gifts and talents, love, light, personality, and destiny, are all held hostage by childhood trauma, rejection, pain, disappointment, and events you haven't let go of. The only way to free these beautiful gifts is to heal and become whole. There are many ways to do this, but I am a big advocate of therapy. I started diving deeply into therapy when my wife and I welcomed our son, AJ. The moment my son entered this world, I became extremely triggered and filled with so much anxiety. Growing up in a single-parent household where my mom had to be both mom and dad, I never had the example of a strong male role model. With that, I grew up with a lot of insecurities around the idea of what manhood is. I had been given the responsibility of raising a son, but how could I possibly do that when I grew up without the person who was supposed to show me how to be a man? All the trauma I thought I had overcome rushed to the surface when AJ entered the world. The pain, the rejection, the abandonment issues, all of these things needed to be addressed if I was going to be the father I wanted to be. As the saying goes; *"the only way out is through"*. So I got myself into therapy and I made a commitment to face these feelings head-on, no matter how painful it was. I would show up every single week and make damn well sure I was a father who could guide my son, who could show him what healthy masculinity looks like, and who could be the example of how to carry yourself in the world in a way that will make your life enjoyable, impactful, and meaningful. AJ was my driving force, but what I didn't realize is he was the catalyst for my next evolution as an influencer. Everything I was doing in therapy was to make me a better father, but it also made me a better human, a better creator, and it made me even more connected to my purpose. Your life experiences, both positive and negative, are there to help you grow. When you view them as such, your influence grows too. But, you have to let go of the old stories, the pain, the excuses, the negativity, and the blame, so you can rise to the next level. Working on yourself is just as important as working to be successful. No matter how much you chase success, you can never outrun the things that keep you from being whole. You can't put a bandaid on the areas of your life that need deeper care, you have to deal with those issues. Don't ignore your triggers, be grateful for them, for they are messengers of the unhealed parts of yourself. As high-performance coach Brendon Burchard said; *"If you carry pain to the next level then trust me, the floor will drop out on you soon. Release that pain and ascend."*

Gift Yourself The Apology You Won't Get From Others

A few years ago, I did something radical. I had been carrying around the pain of someone close to me leaving unexpectedly, and I finally realized I had to heal to stop the issues that pain was causing from taking over my life. I had carried the hurt with me for years and I was tired of giving this person real estate in my thoughts and my spirit. I wanted to be whole, free, and me again. That radical act was something I'd never done before. I wrote a letter to this person expressing my disappointment and pain. You may have heard of this technique before, you do not send the letter, but you allow yourself to say the unsaid. But, I took it one step further. I wrote a response letter. I knew I was never going to hear the words I so desperately needed to hear from them in real life, so I took it upon myself to make sure I got them. I wrote to myself as if I were them, and I wrote the apology I needed to finally move on. It felt so real that it brought tears to my eyes. The mind is a powerful thing, it will believe what you want it to. The pain you've experienced, and the traumas in your life are not permanent. You can heal them by making a decision today that you are no longer going to be tormented by your past. You don't have to allow your history to keep you from your destiny. I healed my life and created the response I needed that I would have never gotten if I had not become an active participant in my healing. Sometimes, the closure and healing you are waiting for someone else to give you will never come, you have to create that for yourself. Author Louise Hay says; *"You have the power to heal your life, and you need to know that. We think so often that we are helpless, but we're not. We always have the power of our minds...Claim and consciously use your power."*

The more you heal, the more your authentic self begins to unfold. As you build your inner brand, you will need to let go of past pain so you can learn and grow from the lessons it provided you with. These lessons ultimately become part of your service in life. So, what are you willing to do to become the influencer you were born to be? Maybe it's therapy, maybe it's time to walk away from a toxic relationship.

Perhaps you are ready to discover your relationship with God. Or it could be writing a healing letter like I did. What about writing a letter to your younger self? Every day you

> YOUR PAIN MAY NOT HAVE BEEN YOUR FAULT, BUT THE HEALING IS ALWAYS YOUR RESPONSIBILITY.

have a choice. You can hold on to anger, bitterness, grudges, and thoughts of revenge, or you can give yourself the gift of healing so a greater influencer can emerge from you. Remember, forgiveness is never about the other person, it's about you. As the saying goes;

"Your pain may not have been your fault, but the healing is always your responsibility."

Is God In That Coat?

On a cold snowy day in Manhattan, I walked to the nearby Chase Bank one block away from the hotel I was staying at. I needed some cash to leave a tip for the housekeeper who serviced my room. As I was about to enter the bank, I could see a homeless man lying flat on his back on the window ledge. A woman placed a one-dollar bill underneath this man's head. As I walked past her, I locked eyes with her and gave her a thumbs-up. I was moved by her act of kindness and the example she had set. This moment called me to step up to my own influence, what was I going to do? You see, living a life of purpose is not about living for moments of extraordinary influence, it is seizing the everyday moments you are given to be of service, no matter how big or small they might be. So I decided to follow the example of this woman. I withdrew money from the ATM, walked over to the man, and whispered; *"Hey, I just wanted to leave something for you."* as I tucked the money underneath his head. He awoke from his slumber, and he said something that melted my heart; *"Brother, God is in that coat".* I was bundled up trying to keep warm, just like he was. We chatted for a bit, exchanged names, and I told him to keep warm. He taught me a powerful lesson that day. Influence is about the God that is in the coat. It's about the generosity in your heart. It's the small acts of kindness and humanity that drive your platforms. Your authentic influence is about the spirit and intention behind your posts, the love that is within everything you do and share. It's in your compassion. No matter what your outward appearances are, is God within?

Every day, as you move about the world, you are given tiny opportunities to use your influence for good but they are often missed because, in the real world, they don't come with a like button. How many people do you come into contact with each day in an offline setting that could receive your blessings? Think about the ripple effect one small act of kindness has, and how huge your influence can be if you infuse your purpose into absolutely everything you do, everywhere you go, and everyone you meet. The term "influencer" has been coined in an online world, but it transcends social media in a powerful way that should never be underestimated. A true purpose-driven influencer isn't interested in documenting their influence, the reward of likes, comments, and social approval isn't what motivates them. It's seeing the real-life, tangible moments that literally change someone's life. For all I know, the money the homeless man received from me and the kind woman that day could have saved his life. It could have fed him when he was close to starving, it could have bought him a night in a shelter, out of the cold, and it could have gotten him clean water for a few days. When you ground yourself in the reality of the offline world, you humble yourself. You make sure you never forget what it's really about. The free hotel stays, the luxury travel, the brand deals that so many influencers chase and use as a marker for success, it's not real. Your offline presence, that can't be faked. How are you influencing your family, your community, your marriage, or your friendships? How are you influencing strangers that you interact with in the street?

Instagram may boast 2 billion active monthly users, but there is a world out there of 8 billion people who are all available to your influence. Don't forget to keep God on the inside. When it's your offline presence that is the most powerful, you'll experience greater influence, greater success, and most importantly, greater fulfillment.

> EVERY DAY, AS YOU MOVE ABOUT THE WORLD, YOU ARE GIVEN TINY OPPORTUNITIES TO USE YOUR INFLUENCE FOR GOOD BUT THEY ARE OFTEN MISSED BECAUSE, IN THE REAL WORLD, THEY DON'T COME WITH A LIKE BUTTON.

Take Action:

Now it's time to get intentional about your inner brand. Remember, building your inner brand as a purpose-driven influencer is an ongoing process. These actions are a starting point that can guide you in creating your foundation for lasting and meaningful influence.

1. **Complete An Authenticity Assessment:** An Authenticity assessment is really designed to protect your purpose and keep you on purpose. Create time to do a daily check-in with yourself. For me, that looks like a heart check-in. I survey the landscape of my heart, making sure that my intentions for what I am doing are right.

2. **Create A Purpose-Driven Influencer Mission:** Clearly articulate your mission as an influencer. What posi-

tive impact do you want to make? Defining your mission helps you stay focused on meaningful goals and contributes to building a purpose-driven brand.

Ex: My Mission: To be a positive force in the lives of those around me, live a life of purpose, and inspire others to do the same.

3. **Prioritize Soul Health Practices:** Soul health is the new wealth. Incorporate intentional practices for soul health into your routine. This could involve seeking therapy, finding a mentor, or hiring a coach to guide you through emotional well-being. Consistently investing in your inner self not only fosters personal growth but also strengthens the foundation for lasting success as a purpose-driven influencer. This scripture reminds me to turn inward and to not only focus on my physical health but also my spiritual health: *"Beloved, I pray that you may prosper in all things and be in health, just as your soul prospers."* III John 1:2 NKJV

PART TWO

The Making Of An Influencer

Chapter Four
Purpose Over Popularity

"Leadership is not a popularity contest; it's about leaving your ego at the door. The name of the game is to lead without a title."

—Robin Sharma

When you think about living a life in total alignment with your purpose, what comes to mind? I can tell you now, that if you're thinking about becoming a household name, having hundreds of thousands of followers, and being offered extravagant and grand opportunities full of glitz and glamor, you're on the wrong track. Purpose has nothing to do with any of those things. Purpose is about doing something meaningful with your life. Purpose is what fills your soul and makes waking up every single day worthwhile because you get to make a difference with what you are called to do. A purpose-driven influencer must understand that when you share your gifts with the world, it has meaning no matter the size of your audience, and no matter the feedback you get. Purpose is unique to each individual, and it is the secret to happiness and fulfillment. It is what makes your work significant, the type of work that will inspire people to reach out and tell you how much you have helped them. I would rather find fulfillment in inspiring one follower with something deeply meaningful than in inspiring a million with something superficial. Your power is found in your purpose. We can't tap into our power without first connecting to the meaning of our existence. One of life's most pressing questions is what am I meant to do in this world? We were wired to have meaning. Until we find some sense of purpose in life, life will never be fulfilling or make sense. So we can go ahead and quote fancy sayings, and post them on social media, but until we know our purpose, we end up scrolling our lives away looking at everyone living in theirs.

Some people know that power, maybe you are the influencer who somewhere along the journey lost your motivation to create, but that spark and purpose inside of you is still present and you can get back to the wisdom of your true self and rediscover your bliss. I'm here to tell you that the light that has existed within you since the moment you were born, is still there, it might be flickering, but it is there, your purpose, and power.

> I WOULD RATHER FIND FULFILLMENT IN INSPIRING ONE FOLLOWER WITH SOMETHING DEEPLY MEANINGFUL THAN IN INSPIRING A MILLION WITH SOMETHING SUPERFICIAL.

Follow Yours GPS: Guiding Purpose System

Discovering your purpose often lies in what you love to do. T.D. Jakes wisely said, "If you can't figure out your purpose, figure out your passion. For your passion will lead you right into your purpose." We all have an internal GPS, our "Guiding Purpose System." Similar to a GPS guiding you to your destination or redirecting you when you've taken the wrong route, your Guiding Purpose System is there to be your life guide. Everyone is born with this inner compass. Now, with an awareness of my purpose, it's evident that the things that interested me most as a kid, the activities that excited me, and the classes and assignments in school that captivated me, are now part of my purpose in some capacity. My Guiding Purpose System has always led me towards my purpose. I have a childhood secret – my grandmother doesn't know. When I was younger, I used to take her cassette tapes with sermons and hymns, find an empty room, lock the door, and let my imagination take over. I would record myself speaking over them as if I were an amazing speaker addressing large audiences around the world. What would make a little kid go hide in a room to record himself speaking if public speaking was not in his future? That is not an accident. One powerful success principle I stumbled upon is 'Act As If.' Recall the days of childhood make-believe – you've got the skills to apply this idea to your life. Acting as if means behaving like the person you want to become. When you talk, act, feel, and behave like your desired self, it signals your brain's Reticular Activating System (RAS). This mental tool helps you focus on finding the people and resources that will guide you to becoming the best version of yourself. One of the many ways our GPS (Guiding Purpose System) directs us is through excitement. I believe we know our purpose based on the excitement that we feel. As Abraham Hicks points out, "If you're not excited about it, it's not your path."

One hot summer's day in my youth, I remember being at my friend's house. Four teenage boys got tired of playing video games and, as teenage boys do, decided to shoot a rap video. We put our creative minds together to try and make this video look as professional as we could, on a very small budget. We created an awesome backdrop for the video with bedsheets, our fake microphones were created with paper and black duck tape, and outfits curated from our collective wardrobes. Thanks to my cousin, who at the time, was the only musically gifted one, we had an instrumental for the song which we wrote together. We were ready. We had rehearsed, the stage was set, it was go time. The only thing left on the checklist was to get the camera ready, which I was in charge of. I recall something transcendent happening to me as I was setting up the camera. We did a small test shot and played it back to see how we all looked. All I know is that there was this feeling of unspeakable joy that came over me and I could feel the hairs on my skin rise. Ever since that day, I have been enamored with visual media, storytelling, watching interviews, and seeing myself speak on camera. At the time, I did not have a name for it, but I knew I really enjoyed it. That moment in that house with my friends, shooting that video, felt equivalent to when you hear athletes say; *"The day my mother or father put that basketball in my hand at 5 years old, I knew this was what I wanted to do with my life."* The very thing that captivated me as a teenager is now part of the work I do for my purpose. Think that is pure coincidence? I don't think so, just the universe working anonymously. Signs always follow purpose.

Take a deep look into your life. What are some recurring themes, and curiosities? What are some interests that move your soul that you just can't explain? Here is another question, what are some things you do that you love that make you lose track of time? Let me use myself as an example. I can read motivational quotes all day long, I can read self-help books, and listen to podcasts that help me improve my life limitlessly. I love to encourage people, that is my passion and it makes me so happy when I help people get breakthroughs in their lives. When something I post on social media resonates with my followers so deeply that I get a DM thanking me for how my post has helped them, I know I can spend the rest of my life doing this even if I never receive a compliment or get paid for the value I bring. Where your passion is, that is where you will find your purpose and power. That is your place of assignment. I read a quote a while back that shed some great insight on how to recognize your purpose. It reads, *"The things that excite you are not random. They are connected to your purpose. Follow them."* If you aspire to be an influencer but don't know where to begin the journey, the best place to discover who you are doesn't begin with the persona of an influencer, the real power begins with your purpose. For my influencers who forget their power at times, that includes me, the reason we forget and have to remind ourselves of it, is because we have taken our eye off our purpose. An obsession with what other influencers are doing will always blind you to your own power. Success is not defined by the influencer next to you, success is defined by the purpose that lives within you. Don't let comparison make you forget your own gifts, your own power, and the unique difference you were made to make in this world.

My Shift To Significance

Do you know the difference between success and significance? A lot of people believe they are successful based on the things they have acquired. The houses, cars, and all the material things the world can offer. I remember having a conversation with a very wealthy man, he surprised me by looking me in the eyes and telling me; *"Jimmy I have all the cars and all the houses, but I am still not happy."* He was successful, but he wasn't significant. It was John C Maxwell that said; *"Success is when I add value to myself. Significance is when I add value to others."*

In 2011, I set out for Haiti to give back. I aimed to provide aid, share hope, and make a difference in the lives of those facing adversity. Little did I know that Haiti and its resilient children would give me something far more valuable—a transformation into a person of significance.

As my family and I distributed food, clothes, and school supplies, the Haitian community shared not only their needs but also their resilient spirit. In their strength, I found inspiration. It wasn't just about what I could give; it was about who I could become during my time there. The mission trip to Haiti gifted me a profound shift in perspective. I thought I was there to help them, but, in reality, they were helping me. Their lessons helped me to redefine success. This life-changing experience ignited a lifelong commitment to living a life of meaning and impact.

Tony Robbins said; *"Success without fulfillment is the ultimate failure"*. Instead of chasing empty pursuits, my achievement is now measured by how many lives I can touch. I had to make my life about something greater than myself. I needed a greater pull on my life instead of the temporary high of achievement that wears off eventually because living a life of significance is the only way to be truly fulfilled. Now, I define success and happiness as knowing my purpose in life, developing my God-given potential, and adding value to the lives of others.

Let's take a look at the advantages and disadvantages of significance and success:

Success limits Your Influence:

- You can never get enough. No matter what you achieve, you are constantly on a chase for more.

- Success has an expiration date. As Denzel Washington said; *"You will never see a U-haul behind a hearse"* On the day you die, success ends.

Significance Fulfills You:

- Significance fills your internal cup. It satisfies your soul in ways that success will never be able to.

Living your life with significance brings you peace knowing that you lived life intending to make a difference.

- Significance is about legacy. Significance will always outlast you. Long after you are gone, your impact and contribution will still be felt by others.

What Fatherhood Taught Me About Purpose

Becoming a father was the biggest shift from wanting to be a success to living a deeply meaningful life. All the silly things that used to hold my attention in life, like the number of likes, followers, and material successes were no longer meaningful to me. God had blessed me with my greatest purpose, my son AJ. Parenthood is the highest form of influence anyone can have. Growing up without the presence of a father left a void that, at times, felt insurmountable. Yet, in that absence, I discovered the power of resilience and self-discovery. Becoming a father became the inspiration for me to break the cycle of trauma in my bloodline. Everything I did not get, like hearing the words I love you, daily hugs, and affirmation, I made a silent promise to myself to provide my son with everything I yearned for—a father's love, guidance, and unwavering support. I turned my pain into purpose and that void into a source of strength to provide the stability and love my son deserves. Every day I get the opportunity to impart wisdom, values, and a sense of purpose. Even during bedtime stories reading our favorite book; *"Daddy's Arms"*, I have found a purpose far more fulfilling than anything else in this world. In the hustle of life, I don't miss the chance to tell him I love him. I love it when I call him over and say; *"AJ I have to tell you a secret"*, I can see him smiling as he brings his ear close to my mouth and I whisper; *"AJ, I love you"*, followed by tickles and laughter. I purposely tell him I love him in his ear because I want him to get it deep down in his spirit and subconscious mind. It's not just a phrase but a commitment to assure him of his worth, create a sense of security, and cultivate a bond built on the foundation of love. I am blessed to have a divine assignment like fatherhood that is going to positively influence generations to come.

Focus On The One

Everyone starts with zero followers. You have to be patient with yourself as you build your influence. Let me tell you now, that very first follower will be the one you remember for a lifetime. They will hold a special place in your heart and they will likely come to mind whenever you reach a new, significant milestone, or get to witness the effects of your influence firsthand. They are the one who started the tribe. If you're lucky, they will hang around and follow you for years to come, cheering you on every step of the way. But even if their journey moves on and your message doesn't resonate with them anymore, they will always be the person who showed you what you're made of. As author and motivational speaker, Gary Vee says; *"Fall in love with getting there instead of obsessing over being there, as soon as possible... The best followers are the first few.. be grateful and start building".* You don't need thousands of people to know who you are or fall in love with what you do, you just need ONE follower, they will catapult you forward in a way no one else ever has. When that first person reaches out to tell you how much you have touched their life, you begin to trust yourself more. It powers you forward and you start to believe that your creative calling will align you with the audience that you are meant to serve. Think about some of the biggest artists in the world, they all started with just a few fans who knew them when the world didn't. There will have been times when they showed up to perform in that little hole in the wall and it was just a few enthusiastic and dedicated fans who loved them for what they did. And even if that artist ends up becoming world famous, their walls lined with Grammy's and multi-platinum albums, they will always remember those dedicated fans who supported them when they were nothing but an open-mic singer. I can tell you this, I know every original follower of mine. They have been with me through social media handle changes, they have seen me grow, get married, and start a family. They know when I take a social media sabbatical, and they are the first to tell me they are glad I am back. I know them intimately, and I appreciate them so much for being on this journey with me.

All you need to do is focus on the one person you can inspire. Show up for that one follower, that one person who needed your message and started your tribe because you shared it. Don't worry about impacting millions of people. Author and speaker Mel Robbins gives some sage advice that all influencers should follow; *"Here is a simple trick I use to ground myself before every speech, every book line, every television show, and every sentence I write. I remind myself: "There is just ONE person who needs to hear what I'm about to say."* When you shrink your focus to impacting the life of ONE person, you'll stop worrying about the number of followers, downloads, likes, views, or how long the journey to your personal success is taking. For the first 42 years of my life, I focused on trying to make an income. It wasn't until I focused on making an impact that everything, including my income, fell into place." When you shift your mind to the idea of focusing on the ONE, everything will fall into place.

Collect Artifacts of Purpose

Traveling is one of my favorite hobbies. I've been able to travel to some amazing places around the world; Thailand, Seychelles, and Greece, to name a few. The day before departure I always feel a deep sense of gratitude that I am able to have these experiences. From meeting with kind hotel staff to connecting with strangers who have become friends. Knowing I'm going home can be hard, so I started a tradition of collecting things from my trips to remind me of those experiences I've had. I've collected hotel keys, kept the kind notes from the hotel staff who have taken care of me during my stay, and gifts I've been given. These little artifacts both remind me how blessed I am and inspire me to keep exploring my passion for travel. Every time I open the little box of mementos, it gets me thinking about where my passport can take me next. As I moved forward on my influencer journey, I repurposed this tradition to help me deal with the very real, very natural doubts that occur along the path. Just as those trinkets from my travels bring me back to how fortunate I am to see the world, I started to collect little pieces of evidence that I was on the right path and following my purpose. It could be a heartfelt message from someone letting me know how I've inspired them, it could be a new connection that inspires me. I have affectionately named them; Artifacts of Purpose. They remind me how fortunate I am to be doing what I love in the world. Every influencer deals with doubts, this is something you will have to accept early if you are going to stay on course. No matter how small or large of a following you may have, there is always that part of you that questions if the work you're doing is impactful, or if you are on the right track. Social media is designed for you to focus on the metrics, but I want you to focus on the mission, always. Without the mission, it's all pointless. But with it, that's what will keep you moving no matter what's going on. A true purpose always brings with it a confirmation that you are on the right path. That is what I call a God wink.

When I receive encouraging DM's, I take a screenshot of it and save it to a dedicated album on my phone. This album inspires and reaffirms my commitment to my purpose.

> A TRUE PURPOSE ALWAYS BRINGS WITH IT A CONFIRMATION THAT YOU ARE ON THE RIGHT PATH.

I can look at it whenever I need a dose of gratitude and a reminder that I can make an impact. I say this all the time, even the encourager needs encouragement and every messenger also needs a message. Every influencer needs encouragement and your artifacts of purpose are there to serve as a reminder that you have to keep going because someone out there needs what you have to offer. Collect them and collect them often.

Here are a few of my Artifacts of Purpose:

"I woke up with heavy feelings today. This is the second message you posted today that resonated and is helping the heaviness dissipate. I want to acknowledge that. I know we don't plant seeds and throw pebbles into other's ponds for acknowledgment, but sometimes it's good to hear that your thoughts and feelings you share matter and make a difference"

"Hey Jimmy! I wanted to thank you- your post consistently echoes the truths that God whispers to my own heart. I've felt God nudging and leading, and you have given me that extra ounce of courage and affirmation to just go for it! I took a leap of faith yesterday and published my blog (Sounds weird to even say haha) but anyways, I'm going to be sharing on there. It would mean a lot to me if you checked it out! Again, thanks for the encouragement you bring, keep it up"

"Just wanted you to know I am a counselor in private practice in Ohio and I have clients who ask for resources for daily affirmation and I recommended your page. Thanks for what You do!!"

"I lift you in prayer this morning. Keep leading, keep inspiring."

Now it's your turn. What can you start collecting to create your own artifacts of purpose catalog? I encourage you to start this right away, it will serve you so well on days of doubt. It could be a text message or DM from someone, or it could be something someone says to you in real life that you take a moment to note down. Take out your phone and start an album, or a file in your notes app, and begin your own artifacts of purpose.

Influence Multiplies You

In the world of sports, there is a common concept that everyone understands; not everything shows up on the stat sheet. Some players impact a win in ways that the average onlooker would miss because they are so subtle, but people who really know sports know it's the subtle things that make the biggest impact. For instance; you have players who are an intricate part of the team who don't get the same level of public praise as the star, but their contribution is equally valuable. They make contributions that will never show up on ESPN, because doing the little things is not captivating enough. Those things won't make the highlight reel.

I believe life as an influencer is the same way. What you do in service to help others won't always show up on the influencer stat sheet. Your impact may not always be seen, but it will always be felt. Don't worry about how your stats measure up to other influencers. Have a service over stats mindset. When you have this perspective in mind, you'll understand that the stats of likes, followers, and subscribers don't tell how great your impact truly is. I used to become incredibly wrapped up in how many people had viewed my story or liked a post but all that did was feed Instagram's goal of getting me to stay on the platform for as long as possible. It kept me opening the app and stopped me from doing anything meaningful. Social media platforms want you to focus on the stats because that's how THEY become successful. But this will only distract you from your mission. The players who play the game the right way don't do it for the stats, they do it for the love of the game, they do it for the love of purpose.

John C Maxwell said; *"Anybody who helps somebody influences a lot of bodies"*. You can't reduce your influence to numbers. You might have a hundred followers, but your influence might be the reach of someone who has a million. When you post something or choose to encourage someone, that influence overflows into the lives of all the other people that person is going to have an impact on. When I first started posting inspirational quotes on Instagram, I used to get so upset when someone would repost but did not give me credit. I was the repost police looking to bust people for breaking the law of social media etiquette. After a while, I just had to get over it and see it as a good thing that my stuff was being shared. Don't worry about people stealing your ideas, worry about the day they stop. Regardless of whether I was given credit or not, what matters is my work was circulating out there. You will never know who is reading your blog and sharing your art. Your influence is somewhere across the globe that you probably won't ever visit in your lifetime. I think that's awesome! In the times we live in now, your influence will travel places beyond your imagination. Think about this, someone is experiencing something you created right now! Just as subtle tactics from the underdog contribute to the well-being of the team, your influence contributes to the well-being of humanity. That's a stat that can never be measured!

Your Legacy In Action

Your social media page is your legacy, so post accordingly. You will be remembered for what you post. If you were to die today, is your page what you would want people to remember you by? Purpose-driven influencers post with intention. I call this PWP: post with purpose. From time to time, I will visit the late great Kobe Bryant's Instagram page for inspiration. One of the things I notice is that the comments on his post are always new. People all over the world are flooding his page with flower emojis and purple and gold hearts. They tell him they miss him, they thank him for having changed their lives. He left a legacy through his page and his life. Dr. Anita Phillips states, *"Legacy will bear fruit that you won't be here to witness."* Your social media page is going to outlive you, leave us with something worth coming back to.

The Responsibility of Influence

When it comes to influence, we have to view it as a responsibility that we have to steward. The more the influence, the heavier the responsibility. Social media has led a lot of influencers to believe that everyone is supposed to have a big platform. You don't need a big platform to have a big purpose. Not all of us are going to be called to have a big platform, some of us are going to be called to lead in small ways because that is what we were built to handle and yet still be impactful. Any wise personal trainer wouldn't begin your program with heavy weights, so why should you be given influence you have not built the strength to carry? In a conversation with Steven Furtick, Pastor TD Jakes said, *"I never even asked to be big, I wanted to be effective, not famous. Famous is the consequence of being effective."* Don't strive to be well known, strive to be well used. Life is about purpose and service. Instead of asking to be big, ask to be of service, ask that your platform be used to change someone's life, and ask to be effective and intentional.

It was Martin Luther King who said, *"Use me, God. Show me how to take who I am, who I want to be, and what I can do, and use it for a purpose greater than myself."* The reason I love this prayer, and I pray it often, is because it's a prayer that helps me to keep my intentions of my purpose pure.

He wasn't praying to have a big influence, he was asking to be used for a purpose greater than himself. Purpose-driven influencers are not

> YOU DON'T NEED A BIG PLATFORM TO HAVE A BIG PURPOSE.

asking to be big, they are asking to be impactful, and if becoming big is part of your destiny, it would be the result of you being effective in your purpose.

Start Living A Life of Significance
Take Action:

- Author Rick Warren said; *"Life is a temporary residence."* I think we all know that life will come to an end one day, but how often do we think about it? One of the most important questions you should ask yourself is what do you want to be remembered for? Knowing how you want to be remembered in the future inspires you to live differently in the present. What do you want to accomplish, what will people say about you at your funeral? I know it's scary to think about the end, but when you begin with the end in mind you can live life with a greater purpose.

- Be the example. Be the influencer who is worthy of following. Begin to strive for a life that when people look at you, they can say they want to be like you. What example do you want to set?

- Purpose before paychecks. Shift the focus from making money to making an impact. Wanting to make money is not bad, but it can't be the thing that drives you. Focus on making the people around you better. Your family, the community, the world.

Don't chase success, focus on being valuable and success will attract itself to you. How are you going to prioritize value?

- Serve the one. Don't get caught up in chasing the masses, who is the ONE person you can serve today?

- Become a student of significance. Read books, do research on Google, and watch YouTube videos on people who made it their life's mission to go after significance instead of chasing success. Study the lives of Martin Luther King, Obama, Oprah Winfrey, Nelson Mandela, Mother Teresa, or anyone you personally find inspiring and influential. Find examples of significance and make them your blueprint for how to live.

CHAPTER FIVE
You Are Verified

"Define yourself radically as one beloved by God. This is the true self. Every other identity is an illusion."

—Brennan Manning

I was a complete novice to social media when I first started using it. I didn't even know what the blue check mark beside someone's name meant. During a very kind interaction one day, in which I must have sounded so clueless, I was informed that it meant the platform had confirmed the authenticity of an account and users could trust it was the real representation of a public figure, celebrity, or brand. It means you are legit. *"Ah, I don't have one"*, I responded, *"I guess that means I am not legit"*. We had a good laugh, because isn't that what we all want, underneath everything, for someone to confirm to us that we are legit? It is human nature to want to be affirmed, we're all wired with the need to feel important. Titles, labels, the cars we drive, the homes we own, and blue check marks beside our names make us feel important, they give us a sense of identity to define ourselves by. When we don't know who we are or are not grounded in a sense of self, we tend to look externally for things that are going to affirm us. People used to spend a lot of money to try and get their page verified. I used to get bombarded with offers from people who were willing to cut me a deal, but when you sit back and think about what being verified is about, there is a worrying factor behind this desire that a lot of people are overlooking. To me, that coveted blue checkmark symbolizes validation, recognition, and, to some extent, a quest for identity. Beyond the superficial allure of a verified badge lies a profound yearning for a sense of self. Influencers often find themselves entangled in the pursuit of external markers, hoping that a blue check, likes, and followers will somehow validate their worth and purpose. Nothing validates your purpose but your purpose itself. Until you understand that, you will never be free of superficial things of this world that give you a false sense of identity. The truth is, nothing outside of you will ever be able to give you this sense of identity. I need you to know that you are LEGIT with or without the bells and whistles. The moment you recognize that you are capable of making a difference in the world with your passion and your creative ideas, you are verified. You don't become legit when you feel that you are good enough to start sharing your art, you don't become legit when someone else validates your creative capacity. Your gifts and talent are divine verification. You have already been authenticated with a great purpose by a higher source. You don't need anyone's approval to verify that you belong in the arena of influence. I am here to tell you that you belong here, and there is room for whatever is your medium of creative expression.

It was Brené Brown who perfectly conveyed this truth when she said; *"Stop walking through the world looking for confirmation that you don't belong, because you will always find it. Stop walking through the world looking for evidence that you are not enough because you will always find it. Your self-worth and belonging are not something we negotiate externally. It's something we carry in our wild hearts. And if we spend our lives looking everywhere we go for evidence that I don't really belong in this meeting. I'm not really an artist. I just do this on the side, it's my side hustle but it's not really a job. If we keep comparing ourselves, you will find exactly what you're looking for. "*

> YOU DON'T NEED ANYONE'S APPROVAL TO VERIFY THAT YOU BELONG IN THE ARENA OF INFLUENCE.

Unhackable Purpose

One of my worst experiences on my influencer journey was when my Instagram account got hacked. I lost everything - all of my posts, my precious photos that held so many memories, and even more devastatingly, all of my followers. The community I had worked so hard to build was wiped out overnight. A complete stranger took over my account, and I watched in horror as it became unrecognizable to me. I felt violated, as though someone had broken into my home and stolen all of my beloved possessions. But more than that, I felt defeated, as though a part of me no longer existed. I had lost control of my Instagram account, but I felt as though I had lost control of my life. As I tended to my spiraling emotions through this experience I had a shocking realization - I had allowed my identity to become so intertwined with my social media presence, that someone hacking my account not only angered me, it hurt me deeply and left me feeling hopeless. I share this experience because I want you to take it as a caution for your own journey. You must create separation between your life and your social media. You must create separation between your purpose and your platform. Your platform is nothing more than a vehicle, it holds no verification of your identity. I hope you never have to go through the, quite frankly traumatic, experience of being hacked out of what you worked so hard to build, but if you do, realize now that your purpose can never be hacked. You can always start again with a social media account, your purpose outlives it. Your purpose can be lived as long as you are living. This is why I make such an effort to help people see the influence they have offline as well as online. Do not be ruled by your social media accounts, they are only a tool to reach people with. They are not who you are, they are not proof of your worth, and they are certainly not your purpose.

Claim Your Divine Verification

One of the biggest lies you are going to have to dispel as an influencer is the belief that you need certain things to validate your purpose and your ability to have an impact on the world. Your creative calling calls you to go out there and create. Thinking you need certain things before taking the first step is what keeps you stuck. You don't need to figure out the algorithm. You don't need your social media page to be verified. You don't need famous people following you or a million followers to prove that you are someone of importance. Our identity is not in the mediums we use to share our work anyway, it's not in the people who tell us if we have what it takes or not, our identity and confidence are in the realization that we are children of the divine and we have been verified long before we stepped foot on this earth. That is your permission to live your creative calling. I need you to recognize that your divine verification transcends the metrics and validations of this digital realm. Divine verification comes from the spiritual realm. The cosmic force that has called and predestined you is far more significant than any trending algorithm. God's infinite wisdom has uniquely gifted you with talents and a purpose meant to influence the world. How do I know divine verification is real? Let's take a look at this bible verse that magnifies this truth. Jeremiah 1:5 states; *"Before I shaped you in the womb, I knew all about you. Before you saw the light of day, I had Holy plans for you: A prophet to the nations - that's what I had in mind for you."* You see, you were born with divine verification. You are called to be an influencer to the world. There is a divine plan for the work you were created to do. We oftentimes forget the divine authority we have so we allow the digital realm to dictate our spiritual destinies. This is how you know when you are not walking in your divine verification. You allow things like the number of followers you have to stop you from creating. Instead, you put your efforts into getting people to see you and like your posts, you buy fake followers, and you imitate people instead of creating authentically from the heart.

You get too wrapped up in caring what people think of you, competing with other influencers, or believing other influencers are better than you. Divine verification is confirmation to you that the universe has your back. This awareness empowers you to courageously live out your purpose, knowing that the divine verification you carry is a sacred endorsement. Now that you know that, you can take up space and stand tall in your divine verification.

> I NEED YOU TO RECOGNIZE THAT YOUR DIVINE VERIFICATION TRANSCENDS THE METRICS AND VALIDATIONS OF THIS DIGITAL REALM. DIVINE VERIFICATION COMES FROM THE SPIRITUAL REALM. THE COSMIC FORCE THAT HAS CALLED AND PREDESTINED YOU IS FAR MORE SIGNIFICANT THAN ANY TRENDING ALGORITHM.

Stop Waiting To Be Picked

When I was growing up, one of my favorite pastimes was pickup basketball. I loved to be part of a team, but getting picked for a team was something I dreaded. I envied the team captains and their ability to have the final say on who they wanted on their squad, it seemed like so much fun. But I wasn't a team captain, and I didn't get to experience this fun part of the game. The wait would fill me with anxiety every single time. I'd watch as others around me got picked, one after the next, after the next, patiently waiting to hear my own name, praying that a pointed finger would land in my direction, indicating those powerful captains wanted me on their team. I didn't even care about being the best, I just cared about being picked. The vulnerability that came from missing out on this opportunity made me so uncomfortable. It was as though not getting picked was a reflection of my worth, not just as a player, but as a person.

In many ways putting yourself out there on social media, or even just in daily life, as someone who has a message and a desire to influence the world is a lot like waiting to get picked for the pickup basketball team. It's incredibly easy to equate the response, or lack thereof, from people with your worth as a person. If someone doesn't like what you share, it's easy to feel as though you are simply not good enough. I want you to be acutely aware of this trap because if you fall into it, you will likely begin altering your purpose for the approval of others. Perhaps you have already started doing this, and if that's you, stop right now. The reality is that whether you get picked or not, whether people resonate with you or not, it has no bearing on your worth or the validity of your message. The world doesn't get to decide that. That is why you have to live on a higher frequency where you are not pulled down by stuff like the need for likes, comments, and shares. It's time to vibrate higher and transcend these distractions because that is exactly what they are, a distraction that keeps you waiting for people to come around and tell you that you have permission to play. In the game of purpose, you are the captain and you are the player. You are well equipped to play and express your purpose that you have been called to.

Live Like You're Chosen

When you stop waiting to be chosen and pick yourself, magic happens. The right people show up, blessings manifest, doors open, and like-minded partnerships with other purpose-driven influencers flourish. Your worthiness increases as you live like you're chosen, which creates a higher belief in yourself without begging for validation. Waiting is permission. Waiting to be picked is the posture of people who don't know how powerful they are yet. When you live like you are chosen, you don't need permission to use your gifts, your gifts are your permission. To live like you are chosen, you have to stop living for acceptance and live from a place of acceptance. Living from a place of acceptance is freedom. To me, it's knowing that I am loved by my creator and I can go out into this world and live out my purpose whether someone is clapping for me or not. A lot of us freak out when we are not seen or when we don't get the number of likes we had hoped for on a post, but the most powerful force in the universe, God, chooses us every single day. Put your hand on your heart right now, you feel that heartbeat? That's love. You are here and you are chosen. Let that cultivate a sense of acceptance within you. Your acceptance is not wrapped up in what others think of you, it's in you being chosen. When we wait to be picked by others, and wait to be accepted, we cast a shadow over the light within us and stop ourselves from shining our light of greatness into the world.

Waiting to be picked shrinks you, but living like you're chosen expands you. Waiting to be picked gives people power over you, while being chosen puts you in your power. Chosen people are not desperate for opportunities, they are not sitting around waiting for DM's, emails, or phone calls for chances to collaborate, they go ahead and create their own platforms that allow them to shine. Chosen people don't chase people, their vibe is what attracts their tribe. Once I started attaching my identity to this truth of being radically loved and chosen, I stopped waiting for the world to call my number. I took that energy and confidence of being chosen and turned it into fuel to create my own fire. If you live like you're chosen, you won't ever have to worry about being picked.

> WAITING TO BE PICKED IS THE POSTURE OF PEOPLE WHO DON'T KNOW HOW POWERFUL THEY ARE YET. WHEN YOU LIVE LIKE YOU ARE CHOSEN, YOU DON'T NEED PERMISSION TO USE YOUR GIFTS, YOUR GIFTS ARE YOUR PERMISSION.

Be The First To Like

Being the first to like is my personal number-one rule of self-validation for an influencer. When I first started using social media as my vehicle of influence, I would post something and then wait around to see who would be the first to like it. Sometimes a few minutes would go by and nobody would like it, but I kept checking my phone, feeling more and more deflated each time. I felt like I was waiting for someone to tell me I was good enough. Without realizing it, I had given my power away to the algorithm. So to take it back and use my time more effectively, I created this rule: Be the first to like. I decided that I was always going to be the first person to like whatever it was I created. The first like belongs to you, everything else is a bonus. One of the reasons we influencers create and share our work is because we enjoy creating.

So why wouldn't you be the first to celebrate your work? After all, you are the one who works really hard to create that content, to take that amazing photo, to write that heartfelt caption, it was you who did that wonderful work. Validate yourself by being the first to like and let the need for approval go. Use that energy to keep creating! When the applause is silent, that's when your own clap has to be the loudest. Learn the art of self-encouragement; be your own cheerleader, applaud your efforts, and celebrate your victories, for sometimes, you must learn to clap for yourself. This applies to absolutely everything in life. Being the first to like is quite literally a mantra for self-love. As Maya Angelou said; *"Success is liking yourself, liking what you do, and liking how you do it"*.

> WHEN THE APPLAUSE IS SILENT, THAT'S WHEN YOUR OWN CLAP HAS TO BE THE LOUDEST. LEARN THE ART OF SELF-ENCOURAGEMENT; BE YOUR OWN CHEERLEADER, APPLAUD YOUR EFFORTS, AND CELEBRATE YOUR VICTORIES, FOR SOMETIMES, YOU MUST LEARN TO CLAP FOR YOURSELF.

You Are Enough

You are enough. There is nothing you can do and no amount of success you can achieve that will make you worthier than you are right now at this moment. I need you to read that again and allow that to sink in. Sometimes we get so caught up in accomplishing, getting, and collecting more things. We think that having more will make us more, but hustling only amplifies the unworthiness that lives in us. So when the thrill of accomplishing wears off, we are off to the next race trying to chase something else. All the while not realizing what we're really chasing, something to fill the vacancy in our souls where the truth of being enough longs to occupy. You have to ask yourself, are you really ambitious or is your hustle masking your unworthiness? As a purpose-driven influencer, I am constantly checking to make sure that my go-getter attitude is coming from a pure place to manifest my purpose, not from a place of brokenness. When you abide in the truth that you are enough, radically loved, and accepted, you come to realize that there is nothing in this world that comes from without.

The God-Fidence Of Belonging

The God-fidence of belonging means that you are divinely allowed to take up space. It means you are empowered to dream big and you can be in rooms with people who have greater influence than you without feeling small. It means walking into a room like God sent you. You know that in the multitude of influencers, you have a voice and a vision that can put a dent in the universe just like everyone else. The God-fidence of belonging doesn't make you better than anyone else, you just don't feel less than everyone else. Arrogance is edging God out (Ego), and God-fidence is bringing God in. The God-fidence of belonging is your creative authority to invent, create, influence, and move the world forward unapologetically with your gifts and talents. Without the God-fidence of belonging, I don't know where I would be. Although I still have to muster up courage daily to live my purpose at times, I know I can do all things by living in the truth that I belong. The God-fidence of belonging is also knowing that whether someone gives you a seat at the influencers table or not, you have the power to create your own. It's the God-fidence of belonging that I tap into. Confidence comes from you, God-fidence is knowing the one who lives in you. In his book The Power Of Positive Thinking, Norman Vincent[2] states: *"One of the most powerful concepts, one which is a sure cure for lack of confidence, is the thought that God is actually with you and helping you. This is one of the simplest teachings in religion, namely, that Almighty God will be your companion, will stand by you, help you, and see you through. No other idea is so powerful in developing self-confidence as this simple belief when practiced. To practice it simply affirm "God is with me; God is helping me; God is guiding me."*

What could you do, what would you create, if you embraced and tapped into this God-fidence of belonging?

> THE GOD-FIDENCE OF BELONGING MEANS THAT YOU ARE DIVINELY ALLOWED TO TAKE UP SPACE.

You Admire Greatness Because You Recognize Your Potential

Remember, you are special too. Greatness isn't exclusive to a select few; it's not a rare quality only bestowed upon a chosen elite. It's not for a few influencers, it's for you too! While it's wonderful to be inspired by others, there's no need to be in awe of them. Honor and acknowledge the greatness within them, but always remember that you possess greatness within yourself as well. Instead of constantly looking around and scrolling around, turn your gaze inward. The qualities that make others exceptional, you've got them too. Be inspired by your favorite influencers' talents, but let that inspiration fuel your own unique abilities. The influencers you admire are no different than you. They have greatness in them and you have greatness in you. I recall hearing actress Jennifer Lewis say one of the most powerful things I heard that speaks to our greatness. She said; *"The day I became a star was when I realized that everybody was one"*.

Shedding The False Identity

An influencer isn't who you are, it's something you do. This was one of my greatest lessons after I was let go from my first hotel job due to massive cutbacks by the company. I never separated what I did from who I was, so after losing my job, I lost myself. Now that I no longer had the title to lead with when people asked me what I did, I went into a season of identity confusion and even depression. I was left to wrestle with the question of who am I? I spent a good year being unemployed, and I became even more depressed, gained some weight, and just felt sorry for myself. I felt like my identity had been stripped away from me, but what had really been taken away was the false identity that I built through my job. It had to be taken away so I could come to know my true self. I knew I had to address my identity because I even held on to one of my old business cards, which was a clear sign that I was still attached to what I did. Life has a way of making us come to know who we truly are when we no longer have things to lean on that give us a false sense of identity. Life may strip you of your titles but it can't take away your purpose. You might get fired from a job, but they can't fire you from using your gift. That was a tough season for me because I really worked hard to get to where I was, but it ended up being exactly what I needed so a better version of me could be born. Rejection is truly redirection and I'm grateful for the divine reroute. If what you lose helps you find yourself in the process, then you win. So I tossed out the old business cards, symbolizing the old me, and was ready to embark on this new journey of discovering the real me disconnected from my job. I believe God was teaching me the lesson of detachment. There is a quote that says; *"Detachment is not that you should own nothing. But that nothing should own you"*. It's not that you shouldn't be an influencer with a large following, but if social media crashed and wiped your followers out, you would be ok, because what you do does not own you.

If your job lays you off, or you lose your paid partnerships, or you are not known as the CEO anymore, yes, you will be disappointed, but you are not things you identify as. This is what it means when you are not what you do.

> LIFE HAS A WAY OF MAKING US COME TO KNOW WHO WE TRULY ARE WHEN WE NO LONGER HAVE THINGS TO LEAN ON THAT GIVE US A FALSE SENSE OF IDENTITY.

Plant Your Feet In Purpose

I want you to make a commitment right now. You are going to commit to planting your feet deeply in your purpose. So deep, that the greatest storm the world has ever seen couldn't uproot you. When you are firmly grounded in your purpose as an influencer, you become a sturdy tree planted deep in your values and mission. Being firmly planted in your divine purpose shields you from the allure of mirroring others merely for the sake of trends or temporary popularity. You need to stay focused completely on your message, so it's vital to create a solid foundation that will keep you from the gravitational pull of conforming to what the rest of the influencer world may be doing.

You might witness other influencers engaging in flashy trends, doing what seems cool for the moment. And if a trend happens to make sense for your personal message, hey, have fun! But be rooted in your purpose FIRST. Creating from the foundation of purpose is your anchor. Not everything is going to be aligned, plant your feet in purpose and be unmovable.

Do A Validation Detox

Detoxing is a powerful life practice. You've probably heard about detoxing your body, but in my experience, it goes a lot further than that. You also have to detox your mind, your beliefs, your habits, and your routines. When you eliminate toxins from your body, you enjoy better physical health. When you remove distractions and temptations from your environment, especially online, you enjoy a healthier and stronger connection to your purpose, identity, and spirit. This form of detoxification is all about releasing yourself from the need for approval. It's about building yourself up and reclaiming your power. You are going to need to purge any desire you have for approval from family members, significant others, friends, and those all-important strangers on the internet. Yes, it's nice to have support for your dreams, but you don't need it. It's nice to have compliments and tons of likes on social media, but you don't need them. If you are feeling the ill effects of the need for external approval, it's time to fire up a detox!

Perhaps you will tell your followers that you are closed for spiritual maintenance and take some time offline to focus on the internal work. Set yourself a 90-day validation detox challenge. I have done this myself many times. I take 90 days to dedicate myself to building myself up without influence from anyone else. Every time I do this, I experience profound and life-changing lessons. The biggest takeaway every single time is that I have everything I need to succeed already within me. The power I have to live out my purpose and leave my mark on the world comes from right inside me. I'm in the driver's seat, I'm the captain of the ship. Nothing anyone could say or do could ever impact my own ability to carry out the very things I was put on this planet, in this body to do. The same is true for you. While going through the process of eliminating the validation toxins that were blocking my creativity, healing, purpose, and growth, something powerful happened. I realized that if you feed yourself with self-validation, you starve the need for validation from others. Validation is for parking, not for purpose! As Caroline Myss once said; *"Where you do not seek or need approval, you are at your most powerful"*. Maybe you don't need a validation detox if this is not something you struggle with, but if this hits home right now, let's do the challenge that will help you fortify the belief in your ability to give yourself what you need. I did a 90-day detox, but you can start with 30 days and add more days if you feel you need them. What you will discover during this challenge is that you don't need people's validation to be the fuel for your purpose, you are that fuel. So here is what I want you to do: I challenge you for the next 30 days, don't tell anyone what you are up to, just fall back. Go to work on your goals by yourself, for yourself. No announcements, no text messages, learn to build yourself up in your own little self-validation bubble. Take inspiration from the saying; *"work hard in silence and let success make the noise"*. Sometimes, when your dreams are in the conception stage, they are too sacred to share. You have to be discerning with when and who to share them with, not everyone is going to be happy for you or have your best interests at heart. So get to work in private. Anytime you accomplish something or get new ideas, keep it to yourself. Celebrate yourself, clap, say those affirmations in the mirror, dance, blow a kiss to yourself, give yourself a pat on the back, pray for yourself longer, and take yourself on a solo date.

Do what you need to do, you have permission to make this personal journey all about you. As you commit to this reconditioning process, I know it's going to work miracles in your life that will elevate you to a different space mentally, emotionally, and spiritually.

> IF YOU FEED YOURSELF WITH SELF-VALIDATION, YOU STARVE THE NEED FOR VALIDATION FROM OTHERS.

A Prayer For You

Take Action:

Copy out this prayer. You may want to handwrite it, you may prefer to type it out and use graphics to decorate it. But I want you to have this prayer visible and accessible to you every day during your purpose-driven influencer journey. Recite it every day, and allow it to remind you that you are verified because you exist. Allow it to remind you that you are capable because you are breathing. Allow it to be your anchor, and your daily affirmation of commitment to your true, divine purpose.

"*God, I thank you that you are bringing me to a greater understanding of your love for me every day. The eyes of my heart are being opened to this wonderful and glorious truth of being radically loved. I thank you that I am starting to see myself as you see me when I take steps of faith toward the highest version of myself. I am not inadequate; I am well equipped and powerful beyond measure to do great things that you have predestined for me to do. Thank you for holding up the mirror of potential that shows me how powerful of a creator and influencer I am. And when I don't see myself, I pray that you remind me of my greatness. I am divinely verified and authenticated in your love, not in people's validation. I thank you that I was born to create and make a difference in this world with my gifts. Thank you for making space for me to do that. I carry myself with this supreme confidence and energy in all that I do. And with this God-fidence, I step boldly into the best version of myself today and every day. There is nothing I can't do, there is nothing I can be, because I am loved. Amen!"*

PART THREE

Your Path To Elevation

Chapter Six

Run Your Own Race

"Comparison is the thief of joy."
—Theodore Roosevelt

It's human nature to compare ourselves to others. Our brains are hard-wired to fit in, it's a survival instinct. But as the modern world continues to evolve, there are more and more opportunities to compare yourself to a much wider variety of people. We travel more, we go out more, modern jobs introduce us to people we'd never meet in our everyday lives, and of course, social media puts us in touch with billions of people all over the globe. We're bombarded with comparisons, and it can make you feel terrible.

Despite knowing it's not good for our happiness and mental health, we can't help but compare our lives, jobs, looks, number of followers, relationships, cars, houses, and everything in between. What we fail to realize is, we're only getting a snippet of this person's actual life. That person in the boardroom in the designer suit, they could have rented it for all you know. The woman you met on vacation who seemed to have such effortless fun on her girls' trip, she could be going home to a miserable relationship. And the 15-second Instagram story is literally 15 seconds out of 24 hours. What you're comparing yourself to is an entirely fabricated version of someone else's life, because you don't know them. You're making a whole range of assumptions about them based on one experience.

Like I said, it's human nature to compare. It's very difficult to escape it, but you can manage it. This is the reason I turn notifications off of my phone. I don't want to be bombarded with status updates of what people are doing with their lives every second of the day. You don't need constant reminders of those influencers who seem to be doing better than you. They have more followers, the aesthetic of their content is better, they have flawless bodies, perfect happy families, are thriving entrepreneurs, or moms who balance everything effortlessly. In small doses, they may inspire you, but if you're constantly consuming their 15-second curated stories, they will altogether make you feel inadequate to the point where you begin to question your own creative capacity. Have you ever logged on to social media for the day feeling good and positive, but in a matter of seconds the good vibes are gone? Seeing that one post of someone celebrating their success has thrown you off your game, negativity has gripped you, and now you are ready to throw your phone across the room. Social media has amped up the comparison trap to a level we have never seen before. Every day you are inundated with reminders that someone is living their best life. Another person got engaged while you are still single, a person just took an exotic trip to Bali, this person got a new car, and you got five likes on a post while a popular influencer got one thousand likes on a similar post, and the cycle of comparison seems to never end. It rattles my brain. Just think about how a small device in the palm of our hands can have so much power over us. Be honest, you know you have been an Insta stalker at least once or twice, checking in to see how your stats measure up against other influencers out there. I've succumbed to it myself. But you don't have to be trapped by comparison, you could be free to scroll without being triggered by what you see. You don't have to fall victim to the voice in your head telling you that someone's life is better than yours. The people who are more successful and have more influence are simply people who started earlier than you. So whenever I'm caught in comparison I remind myself of this saying, *"Don't compare your chapter one to someone else's chapter 20"*. We compare our lives with people who have more success and influence and we fail to think about all that it took for them to get where they are today. You might see the result of their success on social media, but you didn't see the journey towards that success. And to be honest, we have no business comparing our lives to others if we are not willing to do what they have done to have what they have. Run your own race. As Bob Goff said, *"We won't be distracted by comparison if we're captivated with purpose"*.

The Highlight Reel Syndrome

One of the biggest Achilles heel of influencers is a condition I like to call The Highlight Reel Syndrome (THRS). It's the cause of much suffering for us creatives. The belief that the life people post about is perfect, although we know there is no such thing as a perfect life. This syndrome is perfectly described by Steven Furtick who once said; *"The reason we struggle with insecurity is because we compare our behind-the-scenes with everyone else's highlight reel"* This is so true, what we see is only part of a bigger picture.

I am a huge basketball fan. I wish I could watch every game, but I can't. For one, I would never be productive, adulting comes with a lot of responsibilities. One thing I know I can always count on, is my good and faithful sports channel, ESPN, for the highlight of the games I do miss. The purpose of a highlight is not to show me the whole game, the goal is to show me a few clips of the most important parts of the game which gives me just enough information to feel like I haven't missed anything. Some highlights can be very misleading, a player who hits the game's winning shot is the same player who struggled the entire game, but his heroics in the final minutes make his greatness look effortless. This is what the world of social media is, it is just a highlight reel that gives mostly clips of the good stuff. If you go to your social page right now, how much time would it take for you to scroll through before you see an image that reflects vulnerability and imperfection, I can probably guess it would take a minute. On the days when you are struggling to create because you saw something online that made you feel like you just don't measure up, I want you to remember this; *"Don't let the internet rush you. No one is posting their failures."* As my mentor, Spencer Tillman, greatly puts it; *"We live in a world of images and impressions. Few are willing to peel away the veneer to learn about the substance of a thing."* What we don't see is that everyone struggles, everyone is grinding hard behind the scenes to make things look easy. The person who lost their job, the mom who is losing her mind, the person who suffers from depression but in every pic they are smiling. Believe me, every influencer, every creative person, is fighting a battle you know nothing about. Sometimes I see social media just like how I see a duck in the water, on the surface they are calm, but what you don't see is those feet moving at a rapid pace below. Online, everyone looks like they have it all together, but underneath the surface, behind the curtains of their platform, we're all like that duck in the water, working hard, struggling, trying to make something out of our creative lives.

I want you to know that a single post does not tell the entire story. It is rare that people talk about the struggle, the hard work, and the failures. Even now as I am working on this book, it's almost 2 am, and everyone is asleep but me. When this book is finally released, people will only celebrate the outcome. What they won't see is the doubts I had to battle, and the times I stopped writing because I did not feel creative enough. What others show on social media is just the highlight reel. They share the good stuff, they don't share the bad days and they don't share the failures. It's all about their successes and achievements. This influencer journey is about running your own race at your own pace.

Protect Your Focus

While watching a horse race one day, I was curious as to why the horses had things covering their eyes. After a little research, I discovered they are called blinders. They are used to enhance concentration and focus. Horses have eyes on the side of their heads, so they tend to see everything. The blinders eliminate distractions from behind the horse and also reduce distractions to their peripheral vision. This means they are more focused, their eyes on the prize set before them. I thought this was a powerful metaphor for the journey to becoming a successful purpose-driven influencer. We all need our own set of blinders from distraction. The better we know ourselves and what is likely to distract us from our paths, the better we can minimize these things. With your blinders on, you can gallop toward your calling with concentration and focus. Blinders are protection for your purpose. Audit your life for a moment and think about what keeps you from making progress. What keeps you distracted from being the best version of yourself? Distractions are the enemy of purpose, they are the subtle, sly, slow killer of dreams. You set out to do something, you wrote your intention down the night before, and you are fired up about working on your goals and dream, but then you find yourself on Twitter and Facebook, adding stuff to your Amazon wish list, or looking at all the other influencers on Instagram and now you are jealous and feel like your life sucks. It's so important for entrepreneurs, creators, and influencers to protect their focus. So do an audit right now. Scroll through everyone you follow on social media and ask yourself; "Does this person inspire my purpose or distract me from it?" If they are a distraction, then mute, unfollow, or block. Do the same in real life. Who do you spend your time with? Do they inspire your purpose or distract you from it? If they distract you, then reconsider how much time you spend with them, if that is possible for you. Influencers need blinders too. How can we possibly live a life of purpose if our eyes are constantly drifting off of the work we are called to do? I'm tired of letting what other people are doing distract me from the destiny that is ahead of me. The late great Kobe Bryant is my favorite player of all time and one of my idols. When it comes to the power focus, he is the first person that comes to mind. His ability to lock in, be in the moment, and chase greatness is inspiring. During one NBA finals, comedian Chris Rock was sitting courtside near Kobe. During a timeout, the cameras caught the comedian attempting to speak to Kobe while trying to distract him with his humor, but Kobe did not even look his way once, his eyes were looking straight ahead, sweat dripping, intense as could ever be with his mind on the miss ion.

What a beautiful demonstration of what it means to truly focus on your purpose and block out the noise. He had his blinders on. Do you have yours?

> DISTRACTIONS ARE THE ENEMY OF PURPOSE, THEY ARE THE SUBTLE, SLY, SLOW KILLER OF DREAMS.

Have A You Verses You Mentality

You need to ignore what everyone else is doing. The only person you should be looking to compare yourself with is the person you were yesterday. Your competition is not the next influencer. It's not the one with the most popularity or the most followers. Your competition should be you. Purpose-driven influencers are not in competition with anyone else, their life is committed to outdoing the former version of themselves. The last post they shared on social media, the last blog post they wrote, the photo they took yesterday, the goal is for it all to be better today. It's about having that you versus you mentality and shattering your own limits. Ernest Hemingway said; *"There is nothing noble in being superior to your fellow men. True nobility lies in being superior to your former self."*

When you think about the time we spend comparing ourselves to other influencers, it really is a waste of time and energy. Energy that you could have used to devote yourself to becoming a better version of yourself. I love this great advice by Oprah on the importance of running your own race; *"The way you step up your game is not to worry about the other guy in any situation because you can't control the other guy. You only have control over yourself. So it's like running a race. The energy that it takes to look back and see where the other guys are takes energy away from you. And if they're too close, it scares you. So, that's what I would say to my team all the time: Don't waste your time in the race looking back to see where the other guy is or what the other guy is doing. It's not about the other guy. It's about what you can do. You just need to run that race as hard as you can. You need to give it everything you've got, all the time, for yourself."* Think about it, when you are looking around to see what the other influencers are doing, it means that you are sidetracked from your mission. The only way to step up your influence is to stop looking back, stop looking at the influencer in the next lane beside you, give your purpose everything that you have, and run your own race. Worrying about who is ahead of you, who is behind you, who has

> YOU NEED TO IGNORE WHAT EVERYONE ELSE IS DOING. THE ONLY PERSON YOU SHOULD BE LOOKING TO COMPARE YOURSELF WITH IS THE PERSON YOU WERE YESTERDAY. YOUR COMPETITION IS NOT THE NEXT INFLUENCER. IT'S NOT THE ONE WITH THE MOST POPULARITY OR THE MOST FOLLOWERS. YOUR COMPETITION SHOULD BE YOU.

the most followers, and who is living their best lives, is just wasted energy and focus that could be channeled into creating. We don't even notice, but we take ourselves out of the race of maximizing our gifts and purpose when we are fixated on what someone else is doing with their lives. The only way to level up your influence is to stop looking at the influencer in the next lane beside you, give your purpose everything that you have, and run your own race. It's been said that; *"there is no competition when you're manifesting in your own lane"*.

Less Consuming More Producing

The greatest antidote for comparing is creating. Before I created routines for myself to put me in alignment at the start of my day, something I'll talk about more in the next chapter, the first thing I would do in the morning is check my phone to view the stats of yesterday's post, then I would scroll to look at some of my favorite influencers and creators for inspiration. Instead of grounding myself in my purpose and setting the tone of my day with an intention, this is how my days would start, then I would wonder why I felt like every influencer was better than me. Starting your day like this is the perfect recipe for disaster. It harms your self-esteem and amplifies doubt in your skills and your purpose. This terrible habit of consuming the work of others before I created something to share with the world made me feel like I was never going to get where I wanted to be, it only made me feel like I was behind in life and that I could never measure up. So many of us start our day by being sucked into how many likes an influencer got, the love they are receiving from people, consuming their content, reading every comment, watching television, and surfing the internet and we wonder why we become envious of those who are turning dreams into realities. I will touch more on how to purposely proof your day with rituals and routines later so you don't get caught up with the stuff that easily distracts you from your vision. Understand that there is nothing wrong with getting a daily dose of inspiration from your favorite influencer, as long as it comes after you have devoted time to your own projects. That book that you've been wanting to write, the podcast you've been wanting to start, the course you want to launch. Making the shift from consuming to producing will change your life.

Don't be a spectator of purpose, be a creator of purpose. You got work to do, now go create something!

> DON'T BE A SPECTATOR OF PURPOSE, BE A CREATOR OF PURPOSE.

Celebrate Others Until It's Your Time To Win

Celebrating the success of others is a mindset every influencer should have. If you can't celebrate someone else's success, why would others celebrate yours? If you are unwilling to hit the like button on someone's post or leave a nice comment, why should someone like your post and celebrate your achievements? Don't be the influencer who sees amazing content and sees someone doing well but refuses to acknowledge or show love. Celebrate that person's win! I read a quote that said; *"Until it's my turn, I will keep clapping for others happily"*

Becoming a fan of others is the only way to create abundance and more opportunities for yourself. I know many influencers are struggling with this and it's time to break this mindset and support others like you would want to be supported. I notice all the influencers that I love who are doing great things in this world have one thing in common, they live life with a spirit of collaboration and are in service to other influencers. Motivational legend Zig Ziglar said; *"You can have everything in life you want, if you will just help other people get what they want."* You want influence? You want people to share your message, your post, blog, or podcast? You want to have a great impact on the world? Well, the only way to become that is through generosity. The beauty of this creative journey is that casting the spotlight on another influencer does not diminish your own. The brightest influencers help others shine. You need to practice what I call the golden rule of influence. Treat other influencers as you would want to be treated. Serve other influencers as you want to be served. Support other influencers as you would want to be supported. When an influencer wins, clap for them. Be willing to share the work they have done that has inspired you. If you wish you had more comments and likes, start leaving comments on other influencers' posts. Tell people how amazing they are and how they need to follow their account. If you want a promotion on your job, be the first to congratulate others when they get a promotion. Spread the good vibes and good news about the work other influencers are doing and watch how the work you are doing begins to spread. I am telling you, this stuff works. I'm a firm believer that what you put out into the universe is returned to you tenfold.

The majority of the followers I have have been a result of my supporting another influencer. I recall leaving a comment on a very well-known influencer, who ended up replying to me, and I woke up the next day with more followers than I could count. What if I chose not to be generous with my feedback, I would've never had more opportunities to serve and inspire people with my message. What is getting in the way of people's blessings is their inability to celebrate others. A simple comment on another influencer's page, a compliment to a stranger, or taking the time to send an email to someone you admire can grow your following. You can create connections you never knew were possible and put more eyes on the work you have shared that will move you ahead of the game by leaps and bounds without the hustle. This stuff works in real life too, it's not just about the platform you have online, it's the people you can impact offline. Every day is an opportunity to add value to others, but that requires getting out of your own way. I have seen this personally in my own journey. I have been fortunate to have some really successful well-known influencers follow me. I can't explain why, but people who follow influential people are curious about their lives and the people they are connected to. This means if you are connected to an influencer their followers are connected to you. So when I comment on a post, generous with my feedback, and that influencer replies, or someone reads a

> THE BEAUTY OF THIS CREATIVE JOURNEY IS THAT CASTING THE SPOTLIGHT ON ANOTHER INFLUENCER DOES NOT DIMINISH YOUR OWN. THE BRIGHTEST INFLUENCERS HELP OTHERS SHINE.

comment, the universe blesses me and connects me with people I would have never met before who are now my followers because I decided to honor the work of someone else. It's simple, if you give people what they want, you will get the influence that you want. Life is an echo. What you send out comes back. What you sow you reap. What you give you get. You never know what generosity can do for your purpose. You may not have a platform that can impact a million people, but someone else does, and what I've learned by serving other influencers with a greater reach, buying their books to give away to my followers, and reposting their content, you can take your purpose and platform from obscurity to the masses overni ght.

Bless The Influence You Want

We don't realize this, but when we look at other influencers with resentment, have jealousy in our hearts, gossip about them, whisper under our breath that we are better, purposefully not hitting like on a post out of spite, we won't ever rise to the greater levels in our work and experience success and abundance in our lives. I learned this from Harv Eker, author of Secrets of a Millionaire Mind. In the book, he lives by a philosophy that derives from an ancient Huna Wisdom. *"Bless that which you want"* How do you begin to bless others? You see a person with a nice car that you like, bless that car. You see someone with a beautiful home, bless that home. You see a mother who just gave birth to a beautiful baby and you desire to be a mother one day, bless their family and that mother. Someone got a promotion at your job, be the first to congratulate them. Harv Eker states that rich people admire other rich and successful people. Poor people resent rich and successful people. Purpose-driven Influencers admire other influencers. They don't resent the number of followers they have, they are not threatened by someone's success, and they show love and support. If you are hating on another influencer, jealous of their success, you will never have it. You cannot attract into your life what you despise. So here is what I want you to do, I want you to become a person that blesses others.

The Power Of You

It's ok to have an appreciation for what other influencers do and to allow yourself to be inspired by their work. But inspiration shouldn't lead you to become a carbon copy of anyone. It's wonderful to learn from other influencers, and maybe even implement some of the things they do into your own line of work, but just remember that you have been chosen for a different purpose. You were created with such intention that God made sure there would be no duplication in the world. Read that again, because this speaks volumes to how special we are, that there is not another person on this earth like you and I. You might see duplication in fashion, technology, restaurants, and social media accounts, but there has never been an influencer like you before. Think about it, nobody in this world has the same fingerprint as you, but guess what, nobody in this world has what I call the same "PURPOSE PRINT" as you either. Your purpose print is what makes up your creative DNA. Within that purpose print is your personality, the experiences that shaped your life, and the gifts and talents you have given you. It is through owning and leveraging the power of this incredible uniqueness that we can put our distinctive stamp on the universe as influencers. Author Mike Murdock calls this the *'The Law Of Difference"* The law of difference states that *"Something within you cannot be found in another."* There are some gifts, talents, ideas, and creativity that you possess that can't be found in any other influencer that exists, that is your point of power. The problem with not knowing our difference is that we try to be like everyone else instead of being who we really are. *"Nobody is you and that is your power"* is a saying I discovered on Instagram a few years ago, and I thought it was a cool reminder about knowing my personal power. It even boosted my confidence and made me feel good for a little bit, but then again, that feeling was short-lived. Although it serves as a great reminder, something is missing from this influencer mantra. I'm not interested in social media quotes that just make me feel good for the moment or that incite temporary confidence, I want an unwavering conviction of who I am and the contribution I can make in this world every time I step foot on a platform or log on to one. I know you want the same. To that I say, to really know our power, it's going to require more than a simple reminder, power is something that needs to be discovered. So when we talk about knowing your power, what we are really saying is that everyone was created for a different purpose and there is no power without knowing one's life's purpose. Some people discover their gifts and talents at an early age, some won't discover what they were created to do later in life, everything unfolds in perfect timing. As I said before, I was raised in a religious environment, so the seed of purpose was planted in me at an early age. I knew I was made to inspire and serve but that purpose didn't blossom until later in life. All my life I heard words used like you have a calling, you have a purpose, you are made to do something amazing in life, that sounded great, but I didn't know if purpose was something that was going to drop on my lap, one day I was going to wake up and have this great epiphany to know what I was going to do and how to do it. I figured if God, the universe, had this plan for me, I would just sit back and wait until that purpose revealed itself. Although I was happy to know that I had a purpose, it also has equally brought the biggest frustration in my life, because not knowing how to access something people have told me that I had has kept me up multiple nights staring at the ceiling, hoping, praying for a sign, a glimpse into that purpose. The voice of purpose is never silent, it is always speaking, where the ones who are not listening. I just haven't been listening, paying attention to the clues the universe has been showing me through my gifts tied to my purpose. I was somehow too distracted to see that purpose has been speaking to me all my life, giving me hints, poking me intuitively, in all sorts of ways, life has been trying to confirm my purpose, but I just didn't hear it or notice. Take a moment to reflect, is there anything you've missed about what exactly your purpose and power are? What is it that makes you different from everyone else, even if you are sharing a similar message? This will be one of the most powerful things you can reflect upon.

Knowing your uniqueness is how you run your own race for all eternity because you understand the magnitude of your personal power and no one can ever outrun you.

> YOU WERE CREATED WITH SUCH INTENTION THAT GOD MADE SURE THERE WOULD BE NO DUPLICATION IN THE WORLD.

Spiritual Grit - What It Is & Why You Need It

"Get on your knees and pray, then get on your feet and work"

—Unknown

To stay in your power and on your path, you also need to have what I like to call spiritual grit. Dreaming is the easy part, not giving up on your dream is what's really hard. Dreams don't work unless you do. Dreams don't work unless you have passion and persistence. Grit is a skill that can be developed. So let's explore exactly how to do that. Here are four things every influencer needs to hone their spiritual grit:

1. An Influencer Mentality: This is a positive mindset and outlook on your life. To have an influencer mentality, you have to guard your thoughts against negative forces. There is something called your inner critic. We all struggle sometimes with the voice inside our heads that makes us doubt ourselves. Are we smart enough, creative, fit, or beautiful enough? We transform our minds by the renew-

ing of our minds. If you want to take hold of your influence, you have to take hold of your thoughts. For years, I struggled with the belief that I wasn't smart enough due to my struggles in school as a kid. I had to change the narrative by rewiring my brain to tell a new story through the power of positive thinking. I read positive material daily to override the negative conversation in my head. I used affirmations to raise my confidence and my vibration. The most powerful way to quiet your inner critic is through reframing. We'll talk more about how to do this in Chapter 7. Turn those negative thoughts around by telling yourself that you are great, smart, successful, and capable of doing and being what and who you want to be. You can't be passive with thoughts that don't make you feel good about yourself. You have to serve notice on them and evict them. If you feed your faith, you will starve your doubts.

2. Role Models of Perseverance: The biggest influence in my life is my mother. Growing up with an absent father, my mother had to take on the responsibility of playing both roles. When a freak accident injured my mother on her job, she was forced to take a job as a taxi driver to provide for me and my sisters. I have seen my mom wake up at 5 am to hustle so she could give me a good life. But it wasn't easy for her. I remember having our electricity turned off and we had to use candles to see. One time the water company shut the heat off, so we had to boil water to have a hot bath. My mother never complained, she was

resourceful and always positive. From having candle-lit dinners to boiling water, she always made a way. I never felt deprived of anything because love was the cornerstone of everything she did. She didn't know this, but she was training me and teaching me the skill of perseverance just through observation. When life gets hard, I often think about my role model of perseverance, my mother, who gives me the strength to push through. Nobody gets to their destiny without conflict, problems, pain, detours, and delays. So you need to draw strength from people who are overcomers. Maybe you don't have someone in your life who is a model of strength for you, but you can find that through what I call mentorship on paper, which is reading success stories to develop your perseverance. Before I had great mentors, I read great books. It was Socrates who said; *"Employ your time in improving yourself by other men's writings, so that you shall gain easily what others have labored hard for"*. Read success stories, watch videos of people you admire, learn about what it took for them to succeed, and one day, you are going to look at your life, and someone is going to be looking at you as a role model of perseverance.

3. A Burning Desire: Author Mike Murdock said; *"You will only succeed when your assignment becomes an obsession"*. The proof of love is the investment of time. How many of us say we want to be great, but we don't make the time to study, practice, find ways to develop our potential and practice the habits that would make us legendary in our

craft? We don't take the courses, don't read the books, we don't seek out the mentors, we do the reps, but don't have the type of devotion that greatness demands of us. The difference between ordinary and extraordinary is obsession. While I'm saying this to you, I'm also speaking to myself. I claim to want greatness, every new year I would declare boldly, *"It's my year"*. But nothing would change. Those nice Instagram captions are cute on day one of a 365 journey, it's what you do after that shows how serious you are. I used to think successful people have an upper hand, they don't, they just know that influence does not emerge without effort. When it comes to your life, you can't be lukewarm. You can't be a spark, you have to be a blazing fire.

4. Unleash Your Potential: Webster's dictionary defines potential as this: *existing in possibility: capable of development into actuality.* All of my life I have been told by many people that I have "potential". It was a word that made me feel good, but potential is just a dormant ability. Bill Parcel said; *"Potential means that you haven't done anything yet."* The question you and I should be asking ourselves is, have we done anything with the incredible potential that God has given us? Did you write the book you've been wanting to write? Did you start the business? Did you record the music that you're passionate about? In other words, did you take action? We will all have to give an account one day about what we did with the talents we all possess. Good ideas do not bring success. Potential

doesn't bring success. Using your potential brings success. To release your potential, you must be willing to develop it and start using the gifts and talents that you have. God's gift to us is our potential, our gift back to God is what we do with it.

There Is Room for Everyone To Win

There's space for everyone to succeed. Instead of dwelling on scarcity, think abundance. Imagine if Starbucks hesitated to start a coffee business because of Dunkin' Donuts or if Lyft held back because Uber was already established. Our world thrives on diverse options and services because these businesses embraced their unique voices. Your desire to start a creative journey, inspired by an influencer, is an opportunity to make it your own. In this abundant universe, opportunities are limitless, and there's always room for another influencer to thrive.

Take Action:

1. A purpose-driven influencer declaration: Let's make this declaration together, place your hand on your heart, and repeat after me: *"I happily and easily celebrate others In their success."* Every day on your timeline, you will encounter many influencers who are prospering, growing their followers, and leveling up in ways that will make you feel like what in the world are you doing with your life. Those moments are bound to come, but when they do,

if what you see triggers you, I want you to lean into this declaration and repeat it as often as you need it.

This is one powerful declaration that has helped me a lot. As I go through my morning rituals, I repeat it out loud every day and I can celebrate others without feeling like I'm lacking anything. I also want you to remember this, what God has done for others, God can do for you, and more.

2. Get into the habit and mindset of being a blessing to others daily. Take a few minutes every day and leave a kind and thoughtful comment on someone's post. Send a DM telling your favorite influencer how much they inspire you, and even if you don't get a response back, it's ok, continue to be a blessing anyway.

3. Give more to get more. The secret to having a blessed life and more influence is directly connected to your giving. Find ways to give to a cause, volunteer your time, tithing, tip hotel staff when you travel, and give to the less fortunate. By being a giver, you are activating one of God's universal laws. *"Give, and it will be given to you."*

Chapter Seven
Alignment Is The New Hustle

"Even if you achieve your outer purpose, it will never satisfy you if you haven't found your inner purpose, which is awakening, being present, being in alignment with life. True power comes out of the presence; it is the presence."

—Eckhart Tolle

In this final chapter, I'm going to talk about one of the most important concepts you will need to understand not only on your journey to becoming a purpose-driven influencer but in life itself. Alignment. Alignment, as a direct definition, means being the same or similar to each other. If we think about this in the context of following your destiny and living out your purpose, it means that everything you do, think, act upon, and engage with MUST be the same or similar to your purpose. This can take some effort in the beginning, but the more practiced you become, the easier and more fulfilling everything else becomes.

What does the first hour of your day look like? Do you open your eyes and immediately scroll your phone? Do you turn on the TV to the news channel, or some reality show where everyone's screaming at each other? Are your first thoughts about what is making you stressed or worried? If you answered yes to any of those questions, you can be pretty sure you're starting your day way out of alignment, and once you're out, it's hard to get back in without a lot of self-awareness and conscious effort. The best thing to do is to choose alignment from the moment you wake up, by creating an intentional first hour of the day in which you can engage with the things that help you feel inspired, positive, confident, and ready to go! My favorite thing about alignment is it means you no longer have to hustle. When you're aligning with the things that keep you in a state of stress, everything is harder, including your influencer journey. It can feel like you're hustling non-stop and making very little progress. Being in true alignment with your purpose and your destiny removes that hustle. It doesn't mean you don't have to work hard, but it does mean that you are fully in sync with what you love and therefore the hustle feels different because it has been birthed from your purpose. Early on in my purpose and my use of social media, I used to randomly post things that sounded good that would get oohs and ahhs, but they were not things that were necessarily connected to my heart and purpose. The more I did this, the more it took me away from my calling and took me out of alignment. Instead of having a clear intention for the kind of work I wanted to do and how I would use my platform, I was busy following the crowd rather than having the courage to create my own content. I had to realize that it's ok not to do what everyone else is doing and instead focus on taking aligned actions toward things that lit a spark within me. To be in alignment means that you use your purpose and passions as a compass to guide you. Alignment is about pursuing things that matter to you most; not doing things that will get you the most attention. Purpose-driven influencers set goals with their souls. We invest energy in things that ignite our spirit. We move with purpose and intention, for it's in this alignment that the true magic happens. This is how you stay connected to your truth and remain authentic always. That goes for the partnerships you create, the people you choose to follow, the brands you choose to work with, and the opportunities that you say yes to. Alignment is what dictates all your decisions and your destiny. As it's been said; *"Alignment is about pursuing things that matter to you most; not doing things that will get you the most attention."*

So, how do we make sure we stay in alignment as often as possible? A lot of this chapter is going to be about consciously creating your morning routine. That magical first hour of the day can set you up for

> ...EVERYTHING YOU DO, THINK, ACT UPON, AND ENGAGE WITH MUST BE THE SAME OR SIMILAR TO YOUR PURPOSE.

success or failure. As a purpose-driven influencer, I encourage you to take a few minutes each morning, straight after you wake up to be completely intentional and invest in yourself mentally, emotionally, and spiritually. This is a sacred time to nurture yourself and could not be more important if you are going to commit to being purpose-driven. Social media is always going to be there, you don't need to give it your attention the moment you open your eyes. I have been, and sometimes still am guilty of this. No one is perfect. But going to your phone instead of going within, taking a moment to thank God and the universe for all the blessings you enter another day of life with is only going to put your focus on everything you *don't* have, and that's a recipe for disaster. I believe you have to go inward before you can go upward and you have to nourish yourself before you can be of any use to others. As the saying goes; *"You cannot pour from an empty cup".* Purpose-driven influencers must fill their cup first before they go out into the world to serve their followers.

When I think about what keeps me grounded as a purpose-driven influencer, and what puts me in creative alignment, it's without a doubt

> YOU HAVE TO GO INWARD BEFORE YOU CAN GO UPWARD

my morning routine that I have intentionally created for myself. It's the place I go to at the start of my day before I walk out my door, or jump on "the 'gram" and start posting my life away. It's important to give yourself a few minutes of stillness before the world hijacks your day. A strong morning routine puts you in control. It's how you can "Carpe Diem", or "Seize The Day". It's a way to help you feel centered and create that alignment immediately so that it's easier to stay connected to your true self and your true purpose throughout the day. You will see examples of this in almost everyone who has achieved any level of success. People from all religions, backgrounds, and careers have discovered that a morning routine helps them improve themselves beyond measure. Especially in this modern world where everything is competing for our attention all the time. Schedules, emails, DM's, it's never-ending. But when we take control over that first hour, we put ourselves back in the driver's seat. Then we're able to navigate the day ahead with the most important thing, your spiritual self, nourished, nurtured, and in full alignment. Purpose-driven influencers know they are not just creative beings, they are spiritual beings, and the spiritual is what gives power to the creative life they are called to live. Creating a sacred space for yourself protects you from burnout, removes much of the pressure life can put on you, honors your creative flow, and gives you somewhere you can stop "doing" for a moment, and simply be. When you are an influencer, there is a great demand for the gifts that you have, which is natural because you were created to use them, but when your energy is zapped, or you have stress from your boss or family life, or you're experiencing a creative block, you need to stop giving to others for a moment and refill your own tank. By taking one hour at the beginning of you r day, you fill this tank first.

Every day, I take my aspirations, my creative life, my gifts, and my talents and bring them with me to my sacred space where I carry out my morning routine. I know I can't live creatively nor walk in the fullness of the influencer I was created to be without this. It keeps me humble, it keeps me in my power, and it keeps me in alignment. In the next section of this chapter, I'm going to share my 5-step morning routine, or, as I like to call it, my purpose-driven influencer routine. I invite you to let it inspire your own.

Create Your PDI Routine

To begin with, I want to make it clear that your morning routine must be personal to you. You must fill it with things that make you feel grounded and connected. It could be as simple as giving yourself a moment to take a breath. You could meditate, move your body with a yoga routine, or spend some time writing in a journal. Whatever allows you to get in touch with your true self and have a moment of spiritual connectedness each day. I have found that in my personal life taking the time to pray and making room for stillness has not only given me clarity and connection to my divine self but also enables me to be the influencer I am. It's in this hour that I surrender everything I'm doing to a higher power. Let me be honest with you, I don't trust myself to handle the weight and responsibility that comes with being an influencer without doing this. Just as I talked about in chapter 2, it's not about you. You can't let it be, because as soon as you let your human nature into the arena, the responsibility you hold will crush you. This is a major truth behind a morning routine and a space that makes it possible for the spiritual nature of your being to come through. I pray for influence and I exercise my will to be great by putting in the work, but the thought of elevation scares me at times. I don't want to be the guy who started out using his influence for good but ended up squandering it. It's easy for pride to increase as we become more influential, more successful, more prosperous, and more recognized in our lives. But always remember, influence is God-given. As John Wooden has said; *"Talent is God-given. Be humble. Fame is man-given. Be grateful. Conceit is self-given. Be careful".* You have to be humble and grateful, and you have to make space for these qualities to be nurtured.

A purpose-driven life is about being connected and in tune.

It's also knowing that whenever you are feeling off purpose, you have this space you've created for yourself that brings you right back to your center. When you prioritize this space, you are happier, more alive, more creative, have better direction, and are capable of accomplishing more. Even in the busyness of work, and activity, you can whisper silent prayers to maintain your spiritual connection or to bring you back to that special hour of your time you started the day with. I'll now share just one example of what that hour can look like. But if you don't have a full hour, even just a few minutes will have a huge impact.

> WHEN YOU PRIORITIZE THIS SPACE, YOU ARE HAPPIER, MORE ALIVE, MORE CREATIVE, HAVE BETTER DIRECTION, AND ARE CAPABLE OF ACCOMPLISHING MORE.

Start With A Gratitude Practice

Let gratitude be the first thing you do in the morning and the last thing you do before going to bed. Adopting a gratitude practice can make a huge difference in your overall mood. It can boost happiness and lower stress, and it's been known to improve health. It's a practice that has improved my life dramatically and set the tone for having a great day. In order to see the effects of gratitude in your life, you can't keep gratitude in your head and your heart, you have to show gratitude through active appreciation. Gratitude is more than an attitude, it's an action. When you take the time to practice gratitude intentionally every day, a grateful mindset will become a habit. I start my day by taking a moment to be thankful for all of the things I have in my life. This happens the moment I open my eyes before I even get out of bed and go to my corner of the house where I carry out the rest of my morning routine. You may wish to have a specific area where you go, or you can do the whole routine in bed. Like I said before, it has to be right for you and it has to resonate with you. But I do encourage you to take a moment to be grateful the moment you awaken. It's so easy to get caught up in the things you don't have, or the things you haven't accomplished yet. But gratitude is the attitude that allows you to stay in alignment with just how blessed you truly are. It's what helps you to appreciate where you are, as well as dream about where you're going. Think about where you are in life right now. I bet there was once a time in which you dreamed about having everything you currently have. We can get so focused on what we're trying to achieve and what the next thing is, that we can fail to realize when what we once wanted has manifested. Making time for gratitude ensures that you always acknowledge how far you've already come. You can keep this simple, don't overthink it. As Meister Eckhart once said; *"If the only prayer you ever say in your life is 'thank you', that would suffice"*. I remember when I first heard this quote, it reminded me that gratitude and prayer are about simplicity. Matthew 6:7 says; *"And when you pray, do not keep on babbling like pagans, for they think they will be heard because of their many words."* Less is more for everything, even in prayer. As a kid, when I was being taught to pray, I recall reciting only a few thank yous every night before I went to bed. It went something like this; *"God, thank you for mommy, thank you for my family, thank you for my sister, my friends, amen!"* God loves simplicity and authenticity.

As we get older, a lot of us stray away from this heartfelt simplicity. We think we need an extensive prayer vocabulary and speak with spiritual eloquence to get God's attention. But you don't need any of that, you only need to make a little time.

To begin this practice, keep a journal by your bed. When you wake up each morning, take a moment to write down three things you have right now that you are grateful for. This sets a positive tone for the day and brings you into a space of appreciation.

Affirmations

Affirmations are declarations that something is true. This is the next step in my routine, consciously engineering what I want to be true about myself and in my life. This involves making a positive statement in the present tense about something you are actively working towards. Let's say, for instance, you are working towards your first 10k followers on Instagram, you might use something like; *"I am celebrating 10,000 people who are receiving my gifts and my influence on my Instagram page, and I am so grateful for every single one of them"*. Even though that might not be true at the time you say it, the idea is that saying this every day helps you get into alignment with the feelings of it being true and helps you to believe it is true. The more you believe it, the more likely you are to take the right actions in your daily life so that it actually becomes true. I remember when I first started using affirmations. At first, it felt strange looking at myself in the mirror and speaking these words to myself that my mind didn't believe. But affirmations are like planting seeds, the day you declare; *"I am amazing"*, you may not feel like it, but you're watering those seeds you've planted, and eventually they are going to grow your belief. Muhammad

Ali said; *"I am the greatest, I said that even before I knew I was."* There is a powerful lesson in that quote. Your greatness and your genius are something that you have to claim. Ali spoke his greatness into existence. You have to speak who you want to become first and allow the conviction of that declaration to catch up with you later. He also said; *"It's the repetition of affirmations that leads to belief. And once that belief becomes a deep conviction, things begin to happen. Keep speaking your greatness until you see your greatness. So when negative thoughts arise, I start repeating my affirmations, I am great, I am a winner, I am blessed."* "I am" are the two most powerful words in the universe, whatever follows the two words is going to show up in your reality.

Speak positivity about yourself, your purpose, your life, and what you want to manifest. What do you want to be true about yourself and your life? Take the time to write yourself some affirmations and make them a step in your morning routine.

> "I AM" ARE THE TWO MOST POWERFUL WORDS IN THE UNIVERSE, WHATEVER FOLLOWS THE TWO WORDS IS GOING TO SHOW UP IN YOUR REALITY.

Visualization

You achieve what you see yourself achieving. Some of the highest performers in every arena, from sports, business, and entertainment, have used the power of their imagination to manifest their dreams. Visualization is the technique of using your imagination to create the life you want. Albert Einstein said; *"Imagination is everything. It's the preview of life's coming attractions"* There is nothing complex about visualization, all of us are using our imagination daily, every minute of the day.

The next thing I do after my affirmations is a meditation in which I will visualize what I am creating and what I want to achieve. Visualization is like creating a mental movie of what you want in life. It's as though you can literally watch a show in your mind that portrays you in the exact version of yourself you're striving to be, having achieved everything you could have possibly dreamed of. It's a really fun thing to do, as you get total creative freedom that conjures up the most incredible feelings of joy and gratitude, as though you're already living that life. Take a moment to picture everything you want to manifest for yourself. Hold that image in your mind and expand it. Feel what you would feel if it were real and true. What sounds are around you, what can you touch and smell? Who is there with you? What are you wearing? Where in the world are you? Make it like a scene in a movie and see yourself experiencing what you desire in the theater of your mind. Motivational speaker Bob Proctor said; *"Thoughts become things. If you see it in your mind, you will hold it in your hand."*

Reading

So, we've practiced gratitude for what we already have, and we've laid the groundwork for what we want. Now it's time to engage in an activity that's going to grow your mind and your skill set so you are equipped to go after what you want. Reading is essential for the purpose-driven influencer as it contributes to personal growth, after all, leaders are readers. Make sure you have a good stack of books that you can draw upon for daily inspiration, whatever that looks like for you. It could be an autobiography of your favorite celebrity, a self-help book, or something relevant to your particular area of knowledge. But choose books that are going to elevate your mindset, foster a positive attitude, and empower you to keep moving and keep improving. Read a chapter a day, or as much as you have time for.

Scripting

Scripting is similar to visualization, but instead of seeing something in your mind's eye, you write it down. You get super clear and specific about what you want, as though you are filling out an order form for your desire. With this exercise, you are going to write down exactly what you want and allow yourself to feel how awesome it would feel when you have achieved those things. By writing it down, you've made it real. It's not just an idea in your head anymore, it's a physical, tangible thing that exists in 3D via your own handwriting. This is what's known as writing the vision. Scripting is a method of manifesting where you write your desired reality in the present tense as if your manifestations have already happened. For example; *"I am overjoyed and grateful to be driving my dream car, feeling the smooth leather seats and the power of the engine as I cruise down the open road."* As you do this, be mindful not to get hung up on the "how". It doesn't matter how it happens, that's none of your business. There are infinite ways something can come to you, more than the human mind could ever comprehend. The "how" is the job of the universe, your only job is to believe. Scripting, visualizing, and affirming are all tools to help you believe. Believe that you have received what you asked for, and it will be yours.

As we move through this chapter, we will talk more about affirmations and manifesting your desires into reality. But the non-negotiable prerequisite to manifesting is to be completely, wholeheartedly, in alignment. A strong morning routine is the basis for this. It will set you up for a day full of self-confidence and self-belief that you can be, do, and have whatever is in service to your purpose and your desired life. I have shared the basics of what this can look like, now comes the fun part. Create your own PDI routine!

5 Easy Ways To Create Your Own Affirmations

I live by the belief that success leaves clues. Some of the most successful people in the world are using affirmations, so that's a big clue that you might want to consider using them too. Here are 5 easy ways to create your own affirmations:

Step 1. Get Clear On What You Want

Clarity is everything. The universe cannot deliver anything to you if you are sending mixed signals about what you want and the person you want to become. I set affirmations that are centered on my purpose and the areas of my life in which I am trying to make progress. During the writing process of this book, I set the affirmation that states "I am confidently writing with ease". I wanted to be a writer who didn't struggle with writer's block, procrastination, or lack of confidence and I wanted to stop self-sabotaging. I did that by repeating this affirmation before every writing session to put me at ease and build my confidence. It allowed me to come up with creative ways to tell my story. Take a few minutes to be in silence with yourself, grab a piece of paper, and think about what you really want and who you want to be. Do you want better health, confidence, money, or attract the right relationship? Draw inspiration from your ideal self so you can take your life to the next level.

Step 2. Start With The Words "I am"

Joel Osteen says; *"Whatever follows 'I am' is going to come looking for you."* Whatever follows the words "I am" is going to follow you. We often don't realize this, but we are always making affirmations and agreements. You change your affirmations, you change your life.

Step 3: How You Phrase It Is The Secret

Saying I am going to get out of debt keeps you affirming the debt. Focus on what you do want. Phrase it this way: "I am enjoying living a life of abundance." I went from saying "I am going to be an author" to "I am an author." One statement makes it feel like it is something that is far in the future; the other one makes me feel like I am that now!

Step 4: Energy Is Everything

Speak your affirmations out loud with power and conviction. It's been said that motion creates emotion. When you say your affirmations, add movement, a smile, give a fist pump, have both hands up like you just won something, jump for joy, and lean into the emotion of the words you are saying. You can use what Amy Cuddy calls "power posing", a belief that changing your body language can make you feel powerful. As for me, when I am saying my affirmations, I can feel the difference when I add movement in the form of slapping my chest while saying I am powerful. Now, I don't want you hurting yourself, so you can use some other positive body language to boost the effect of your affirmations. Include words that have feelings, that are emotionally charged like I am happy, celebrating, or enjoying. Words that put you in vibrational alignment as if you already have your desire. Here is something I do every day to supercharge my affirmations: I put my headphones on, play some powerful instrumental music that puts me in a peak emotional state, and then say my affirmations. Talk about all the vibes, this is a good one to try.

Step 5: Take Action

Affirmations don't work unless you do. That's the thing about affirmations, you can say them as many times as you want, but if you are not taking inspired action, working on developing your mindset, and habits to become the type of person that can attract those desires, you won't have any results. Jim Cary famously wrote himself a check for 10 million dollars as a physical affirmation of his intent to become a highly-paid actor. But he also said that you can't just sit on the couch eating sandwiches and expect to manifest. You have to put the work in. Take me for instance. I kept on repeating the affirmation *"I am an author"*, but then I would procrastinate. I was inconsistent, some days I would write, some days I wouldn't, and I wondered why I did not feel like an author. I was not putting the work in, I thought I could speak things into existence without working them into existence. The universe can only do its job if you do yours.

I encourage you to use these tips to create your own affirmations. They are so much more powerful when they are your own words, created from your own desires. But here are four affirmations I believe every purpose-driven influencer needs to get you started. They will help you get used to the practice whilst you think about what you would like your personal affirmations to be.

> THE UNIVERSE CAN ONLY DO ITS JOB IF YOU DO YOURS.

1. **I am chosen for Impact:** I am chosen to make a positive impact. My influence is not measured by likes or followers but by the meaningful difference I make in the lives of others through my authentic self and purpose-driven influence.

2. **I am empowered by Purpose:** I am empowered by my purpose. Each day, I live in alignment with my unique gifts and calling. I don't seek validation; I live with the unshakable knowledge that my purpose-driven influence

creates a ripple effect of positive change in the lives of all my followers.

3. **I am Uniquely Gifted for a Reason:** I am uniquely gifted for a reason. My talents, passions, and strengths are not random; they are connected to my purpose.

I acknowledge and I am grateful for my unique gifts and talents that make me a powerful force of influence in this world.

4. **I am Free From Comparison:** My path is unique, and my purpose is powerful. I embrace my individual journey, appreciating the value it brings to the world.

Stay Connected

"Those who speak in spiritual terms routinely refer to God as creator but seldom see "creator" as the literal term for "artist". I am suggesting you take the term "creator" quite literally. You are seeking to forge a creative alliance, artist-to-artist with the Great Creator. Accepting this concept can greatly expand your creative possibilities."

—Julia Cameron

One of my mentors has a two-word phrase they have repeated to me more times than I can count; *"Stay connected"*. Just two small, but very powerful words that immediately charge me with the level of responsibility the work of being a purpose-driven influencer entails. You simply can't live a life of purpose unless you are practiced in staying connected to that purpose. Or to your higher power, if you have one. I don't believe many people walk this path of purpose without some sort of faith, whether that's a traditional religion or you are spiritual but not religious. Walking with purpose means a commitment to engaging with a spiritual discipline that is right for you. Be that prayer, fasting, meditation, or simple daily gratitude. You need some sort of practice that can bring you back to your center and connect you to your purpose reliably and consistently. Staying connected means staying in alignment. It means consciously moving yourself into harmony with the reasons behind your ambitions, the intentions behind your desires, and the resolution behind your goals. Without these things, being truly purpose-driven isn't possible. And we really don't need any more influencers without purpose in this world. This is why I've dedicated an entire chapter, the longest chapter of the book, to the concept of alignment. That's how important it is. Staying connected has made me a better human, and a better influencer. Purely because staying connected to my purpose is precisely what ensures I am driven by it. It keeps me humble, it reminds me of the real reasons behind my career choice, it keeps my ego in check, and prevents me from veering down the path of vanity metrics and chasing popularity for popularity's sake. Staying connected by committing myself to a spiritual discipline and alignment practice is what has turned me into a purpose-driven influencer. And it will do the same for you. Everything I create flows from this divine connection. I don't always succeed in maintaining this connection, but I will tell you I notice a difference without it. It's like trying to work with a weak WiFi signal. Have you ever tried to work a weak WiFi signal? It's torture. A good WiFi signal makes life much more enjoyable, I know you would agree. Your personal connection to your purpose works the same way, When we try to bring things into being in this world, without spiritual and intentional connection the magic that comes from your collaboration with the universe is missing its spark.

This concept extends to how you connect with others. First, you must ensure you are in alignment with yourself, then you must ensure you are in alignment in your dealings with others. Both on and offline. You may be familiar with the idea that you are the sum of the five people you spend the most time with.

> STAYING CONNECTED BY COMMITTING MYSELF TO A SPIRITUAL DISCIPLINE AND ALIGNMENT PRACTICE IS WHAT HAS TURNED ME INTO A PURPOSE-DRIVEN INFLUENCER. AND IT WILL DO THE SAME FOR YOU.

As humans, we are adaptable and we are hard-wired to fit in with the crowd. This is the most basic of survival instincts that have been engrained throughout our 2 million years of existence. We take on the characteristics, values, morals, habits, and ideas of the people we spend the most time with because we are designed to fit the mold. When you are aware of this, you can be more conscious about who you surround yourself with. Take stock of your five people, do they inspire you? Do they lift you up and support your cause? Do they empower you to be the best you can be? Do they work on themselves and prioritize their own purpose in this world?

I'm not suggesting you need to start cutting people out of your life, relationships are complicated and that is an extremely personal decision. But if you don't have supportive and empowering people in your life, can you find some? Can you join a new group where you might meet people who are in alignment with your goals and visions for life? Can you strike up more conversations online that may put you in circles of positivity and acceptance? At the very least, begin to take an audit of what and who you surround yourself with and ask yourself, does this help me stay in alignment? And make whatever minor or major tweaks you feel happy with to support you in staying connected.

Sometimes, you might actually find that the very best way to stay connected is to disconnect entirely. This isn't as much of an oxymoron as it sounds. When I say disconnect, I mean from the things that distract you from yourself - your phone, social media, the media in general, or anything our modern world provides that can be in danger of taking you out of alignment. As Anne Lamott famously said; *"Almost everything will work again if you unplug it for a few minutes, including you"*. You don't always need to be connected to social media, you get to take a break when you need to so you can reconnect with yourself. Social media exposes us to more ideas, thoughts, opinions, and mental stimulation than our brains have even evolved to cope with at one time. It's important that we disconnect from time to time. You may have a fear that you will lose followers if you do not post for a while, but believe me, they will come back. Sometimes your purpose will call you to take a break. Think about it, when was the last time you gave yourself some downtime? When was the last time you grabbed a cup of tea and just sat with it instead of scrolling your phone whilst you drank? When was the last time you read a book properly? Or invested in some real rest? All the great spiritual teachers and sages have known and encouraged the importance of rest. Connecting to your inner being is more powerful and soul-satisfying than always being on the go. A purposeful life does not arise from a busy life. You need to slow things down a little bit. My most creative thinking happens when there is a slower pace to my life and I don't have a million things occupying my mind.

When my son was born, I made a radical decision. I took an extended break from social media. No posting, no engaging with other accounts, no mindless scrolling, nothing. At first, I had intended this break to be just a month or two, but it very quickly turned into an entire year. It was so important to me to be fully present in this new chapter of my life and I didn't want anything to pull me out of this beautiful little family bubble. I wanted to take in every moment, every sleepless night, every milestone, every feeling and emotion that came with the first year of becoming a parent. I couldn't bear the idea of missing my son's first smile because I was in the middle of recording an Instagram story, so Instagram had to go. I also felt differently about sharing every aspect of my life, becoming a parent makes you look at these things differently. My wife and I became adamant that we would not share our son on social media and that we would keep our home and family life private. I learned a lot during this one-year break, the biggest lesson being that my real influence lay within the four walls of my own home. How I show up as a father is how I truly impact the world and ensure my legacy is one to be proud of. Those precious twelve months with my newborn son showed me a tangible influence that meant so much more to me than social media followers. But to put your own mind at rest if you have any fear that taking a break as long as this would harm your growth, I've come back stronger than ever. Disconnection can sometimes be exactly what you need to become the most connected version of yourself you've ever known.

Surrender Is The Key

> *"You must give up the life you planned in order to have the life that is waiting for you."*
>
> ——Joseph Campbell

There is a final step to alignment and connection I have yet to share with you. I am sure you have heard the saying; *"if you want to make God laugh, tell God about your plans."*

Things rarely work out how we expect them to. Goals are good, goals keep you focused on the end result you are looking to achieve, but plans almost always go awry. That's because ultimately, we aren't in control of how something plays out. God, the universe, your higher power is. So the final step of alignment and connection is always going to be surrender. You have to let it all go. You have to make peace with the fact that it may not happen how you expect it to happen, but keep the faith that it WILL happen. When you are feeling worried, and frustrated, and it feels as though things are falling apart, letting go allows you to invite in the wisdom of the universe. When you let go, you allow life to unfold at its own pace. You can't be late for your destiny, I promise.

I appreciate it's not easy to do, we've been trained our whole lives to be in control at all times. I myself struggle with the idea of surrendering, but if we are going to make progress and move forward, it's a non-negotiable that has to happen. You have to let go and allow the universe to do its work. I know whenever I am feeling anxious about my life, fearful about the future, or concerned about my next steps and who I am becoming, it can feel as though I am doubting God. But then I have to remind myself, these feelings are present because I am trying to control the "how". The "how" is not my business. So I release the habit of control and I surrender to the process, and before I know it, I am back in alignment. As a purpose-driven influencer, expect times when things will not go as planned. Rejections, both from opportunities and people you wish to collaborate with, are part of the journey. Embrace the philosophy of *"rejection as divine redirection."* I faced my share of "No's" while writing this book, but I want you to see these moments not as setbacks but as divine guidance. Trust that the right people will support your purpose. Remember, beyond every rejection, a greater "yes" awaits. Purpose-driven influencers, like you, experience extraordinary blessings and miracles when they choose to trust.

Control will take you away from your purpose, but surrender will bring you closer to who you were created to be. Trust and surrender

REMEMBER, BEYOND EVERY REJECTION, A GREATER "YES" AWAITS.

will take your life to places where worry and control never could, and it'll feel better on the journey! Whenever you find yourself frustrated with the way your life looks, whenever you feel lost or like you don't have a purpose, whenever you doubt that your career can thrive or your desires can manifest, it's time to let go and let God. It's time to surrender. On the other side is a life even greater than the one you've visualized and scripted for yourself. It was Oprah that said, "God can dream a bigger dream for you than you can dream for yourself, and your role on Earth is to attach yourself to that divine force and let yourself be released to it."

It's in your best interests to surrender as often as possible, because when we try to control our path, we often make the wrong decisions for ourselves and stay in situations or relationships that aren't good for us because we fear the change that leaving them will create. But if that situation or relationship is not part of your destiny, sooner or later, you will be forced to surrender it. You may resonate with this, perhaps you were once in a relationship that you intuitively knew wasn't working and wasn't serving you, but the fear of moving on made you ignore that intuition. Maybe the universe came knocking with signs that it was time to move on and find someone who would truly see your light and worth, but you ignored them. And I'll bet that relationship eventually ended in an abrupt or dramatic way because when we ignore these signs and subtle hints, they only get louder until we are forced to listen. The same happens when we are not following our purpose, not taking care of our health, or giving time to friendships that are not supportive or too one-sided. The universe has a way of course correcting you when you are veering too far from your destiny. This is what I call a divine interruption. The sooner you answer the call and surrender to the divine interruption, the smoother the ride will be. We are very stubborn people by nature, so sometimes the extreme has to happen for God to finally get our attention. If you find yourself being nudged to surrender I promise you it's for the better. It's God's plan. Each and every time I was tempted to remain stagnant because I couldn't understand how things were going to get better, something came along that pushed me forward and forced me to level up. I've had job layoffs, rejections, and problems coming out of nowhere, and looking back on them now, they were all leading me to become a better version of myself. That's what a loving universe and God do, they use divine interruptions to activate us into becoming powerful versions of ourselves.

> *"Not all storms come to disrupt your life, some come to clear your path"*
> —Unknown

In 2007 a divine interruption came knocking at my door. I was working for a hotel and my director was riding me hard. She put so many demands on me at the start of the new year because she wanted things to be perfect. We had some big executives from corporate coming in and she was stressed about impressing them. I remember being so overwhelmed one day that I started to have a panic attack. I couldn't breathe. It literally felt like I was going to have a heart attack. I took a seat in one of the hotel meeting rooms, and I called her. I told her I wasn't feeling well and I thought I needed to go to the hospital. Minutes later, I was surrounded by the entire executive team. As they looked at me cocked back in my chair, I whispered to everyone that I couldn't breathe. Someone removed my tie and helped me take my suit jacket off so I could be more comfortable. An ambulance was called and I was taken out on a stretcher and rushed to the nearby hospital. For the next seven days, I was ordered to rest by the doctors. I was burnt out. During that time, I had a chance to be still and think about my life and my next steps, and if striving to climb the corporate ladder was really worth it. The truth is, my time at that job was coming to an end, but I wanted to hold on to it because my title gave me a sense of identity. Although I knew I had been getting weary and wanting to move on for some time, I didn't listen to these intuitive nudges. Eventually, they laid me off, and it was the best thing that ever happened to me. The old adage is true; *"Life doesn't happen to you, it happens for you."* Often, our issues with surrender are not just about our inability to relinquish control of our lives, it's our inability to believe that there is better. I live by the belief that if one door closes, another one opens. And if it doesn't open, it means it's not your door. This experience not only made me a better person, it led me to opportunities that I would have never had if I stayed in a place where my purpose had expired. The final step in alignment is always surrender, you can not possibly know exactly how your path is paved, your only responsibility is to walk it.

Less Doing, More Being

In the world we live in today, so much of the focus is on doing instead of being. We have confused activity for productivity. I have to admit, sometimes I feel the pressure of producing because at times I often convince myself that I am behind time. We tend to look at our destiny as a race, looking at the people who are before us. The truth is, none of us are behind time, we are all moving at the pace of our own processes. It's this idea of having to do more that is robbing us of the pure joy of living our purpose. So many people are doing more but feeling less. I don't want to get to the end of my life only to realize that I added a whole bunch of things to my plate that had nothing to do with my mission in the first place. Let us conserve our energy for things that add real meaning and service to the world. I can see how it's easy to get trapped in the mode of doing because there is always something to do, a to-do list to check things off, the next great book that tells us how to become happier, the next podcast with the life-transforming advice, the newest influencer and guru on Instagram that is telling us to be successful we have to grind more. It needs to stop! Everything is leading us in the direction of doing but who is encouraging us to just simply be? It's ok to give yourself permission to stop doing and just be. This is such a calming and powerful truth that enables us to bring more presence to our lives and allow us to be in the moment. When you think about productivity, the first thing that comes to your mind is probably doing, and I can't blame you for that because that is what we were taught. We live in a world that values productivity over everything else because it's built on the system of capitalism. We're taught that wealth and status are the ultimate markers of success and that we should pursue them at all costs. But what this creates is something called hustle culture. Right from school age, it's ingrained in us all that we have to grind if we're to have any hope of becoming successful, or even useful to society. But it's simply not true. It's something we do on autopilot because our minds are conditioned to do so and there are no examples of another way. When your purpose takes priority, you become forced to re-evaluate these things because what you do on autopilot isn't always going to be in service to your purpose.

This is quite possibly the greatest gift your decision to become a purpose-driven influencer can give you. You get to find another way, your way, a way that allows you to create the impact you desire to have on the world and the life you desire for yourself without burning yourself out hustling and giving yourself over to the grind. Being productive has a lot to do with taking action, but to be truly productive we need to be present. Sometimes, that requires us to stop what we are doing and be still for a moment. Some of my best ideas come to me when I allow space for creativity by simply being s till.

Unleashing Your Creativity Anytime, Anywhere

Having a solid morning routine, a spiritual practice that resonates with you, and a commitment to what helps you stay connected to your true self are all very important things on your journey. But, you're still human, and life happens. Sometimes even the strongest of routines is going to fall short. Unexpected circumstances are going to arise, plans will veer off course, or you'll experience the natural highs and lows of the human experience and find yourself simply unable to connect and unable to create. I'm telling you now, this will happen from time to time and it's nothing to beat yourself up over. Perfection is not the goal, and you must surrender to the human condition. Do not blame yourself when this happens or get too caught up in overanalyzing why it's happened, that will only serve to spiral you further. Instead, when your creativity is off, find something you can be grateful for. Each time I sit down to write a new section of this book, I say a prayer thanking God, the universe, and all the people who are going to read this book once it is published. I take a moment to think about how it's going to help the world, and I allow the magnitude and the gratitude of that to fully wash over me. I imagine the positive feedback, I think about all the people on social media and offline telling me this book is so timely and is exactly what they need to be reading at this moment in their lives. In everything I do, from every post to any piece of content I create, I give thanks for the opportunity to share my gifts. Then I surrender it out to the universe. This allows me to get into the mindset of the people I help and what they need, rather than staying frustrated about where I am. This is what unleashes my creativity once more. Whenever I get frustrated or doubt my ability to carry out the work I've been called to do, I take a few minutes to pause and invite in gratitude. It brings me back to my creative energy every time and infuses me with the optimism I need to soar.

We all doubt our genius at times, but those doubts and fears are not real, they just want to delay the magic that you have been assigned to bring into this world. The idea of being creatively stuck is an illusion. I remember I used to say I have writer's block, I don't have the words to write this book, I'm not a seasoned writer like all the greats I admire, I'm just not feeling creative, and so on and so on. The result of that would be procrastination, then after that, I would go through a cycle of beating myself up for not creating anything for the day. I am pretty sure this sounds like a very familiar path you've traveled before. It was not until I heard an interview with Seth Godwin that changed the way I speak and think about the creative process. He said; *"There is no such thing as writer's block. Writer's block is the fear of bad writing"*. That truth set me free on so many levels. The reality is, being stuck creatively is a lie we tell ourselves because deep down we know we are afraid of making stuff that sucks. Instead of calling out our resistance as fear, we give it a nice cute name like "Writer's block".

There are various reasons we feel stuck creatively. For me, I know I'm the one that always gets in the way of the muse. But here are just some examples of why you may be feeling creatively stuck:

> THE REALITY IS, BEING STUCK CREATIVELY IS A LIE WE TELL OURSELVES BECAUSE DEEP DOWN WE KNOW WE ARE AFRAID OF MAKING STUFF THAT SUCKS.

- You believe you have to be perfect. The antidote to this is quite simply to embrace the messy nature of the creative process. It's not supposed to be perfect. Some days you create a masterpiece, and then there are days where you just throw enough paint on the canvas to be able to say you created something today. That's the nature of the creative game. Either way, you are still a creator. Whether it's building a house, painting for a gallery, writing a book, cooking up a storm in the kitchen, or any manner of creative pursuit, it's going to look messy until it's finished. Don't judge your work in progress, it will only stifle your ability to finish. Understand that perfection is a useless goal.

- You are not consistent. It's not what you create once in a while that matters, it's what you create consistently. In sports, the more you are on the court or field, the better rhythm you get yourself into. That mindset applies to the work you do creatively. The reason we often feel out of creative rhythm is that we are not consistently showing up to play the game we love. The creative reps we put in daily are what give us flow. You can't date creativity, you can't call it one day and ignore it the next. It requires a real commitment. You must marry it and be faithful to it. This is the only way.

- You're waiting to be inspired. Stephen King said; *"Amateurs sit and wait for inspiration, the rest of us just get up and go to work."* You can't wait for inspiration, you have to proactively create the conditions in which it can manifest. Inspiration finds us when we are doing the work, not when we're thinking about it. We can't be amateurs, we have to be pros. Our purpose and creative calling are too sacred and important to leave it up to the ebb and flow of our feelings. Creativity is not a feeling, it's a habit.

Positive Mind, Positive Life

Guarding your thoughts and renewing your mind daily are key practices for purpose-driven influencers. Elevating your mindset is crucial because a negative mind will never give you a positive life. To manifest our dreams, we have to consistently replace negative thoughts with empowering truths. Follow Jim Rohn's advice; *"Every day, stand guard at the door of your mind"*. It's been said that your mind will believe what you tell it, so fill it with faith, truth, and love. Embrace these daily practices to reshape your thoughts positively, aligning them with your influencer purpose.

Your influence will only rise as high as your mindset. I experienced a transformative shift in my life when I started believing in myself, trading lies for the truth of my worth according to God. Many dreams remain unrealized due to self-imposed limitations; thinking bigger and acknowledging your worthiness propels you toward your desires. There is a quote by Marianne Williamson that had a profound impact on my mindset; *"Our deepest fear is not that we are inadequate, Our deepest fear is that we are powerful beyond measure. It is our light, not our darkness that most frightens us."* We ask ourselves; *'Who am I to be brilliant, gorgeous, talented, fabulous?'* But actually, who are you not to be? You are a child of God. Working on my mindset daily has taught me that who you become depends upon getting your thoughts synchronized with the thoughts God thinks about you. That's why I began working overtime on my mindset. Growing up with numerous limiting beliefs and the experiences of my childhood left a lasting impact on my confidence into adulthood. So, I delved into books on changing my mind because I understood that in order to realize my potential, I needed to elevate my thoughts. As the Word says; *"Be transformed by the renewing of your mind."* This journey of reshaping my mindset has been a continuous process, and I've seen the profound impact it has on unlocking my true potential and you can do the same. Much of this ties in with the concept known as The Law of Attraction. This is a universal law that states like attracts like. In other words, being in alignment with what you want attracts it into your life. When I first started learning about the Law of Attraction, I realized I had been using this law by default. We all have because it's working whether we're aware of it or not. Armed with this knowledge, I took time to reflect on the things I have attracted into my life from luxury vacations, checks in the mail, and meeting influential people in the world, to having an amazing partner, great relationships, and even my beautiful son. With this understanding, I could see the events that unfolded that led me to manifest all of these things. Now that I know this law, my goal has become to use it with intention, always. My desire is for you to use this law if you haven't already, and to teach you some simple steps to attract more opportunities, ideas, abundance, resources, and relationships that will help you fulfill your vision and your soul's purpose. This is another reason why I want you to commit to a morning routine and all of the practices I have talked about so far in this chapter. They are more than tools to keep you connected and in alignment, they are tools for manifestation. They are ways to consciously work with the Law of Attraction to create everything you've ever dreamed of. Your thoughts, beliefs, and actions become things. Committing to visualizing, scripting, reciting affirmations, and all of the practices I share with you in this book are all ways to ensure you are attracting what you want, instead of draining your focus on distractions and aligning yourself with things you don't want. When you understand this law and work with it intentionally, you really are cooking with gas! As well as your morning PDI routine, practice mindfulness throughout the day. Be aware of your thoughts and actively monitor them. When negative or self-limiting thoughts arise, say thank you for visiting me and consciously replace them with positive affirmations. This habit helps break the cycle of negativity and trains your mind to focus on empowering thoughts. There is a proverb that says; *"You* cannot keep birds from flying over your head but you can keep them from building a nest in your hair". You are the best project you can ever work on, so feed your mind with uplifting and personal development content. Read books, listen to podcasts, or attend workshops that inspire personal growth and positive thinking.

Continuous learning enhances your perspective, challenges negative beliefs, and fosters a mindset of growth, resilience, and purpose. Remember, transforming your thoughts is a gradual process, so stay committed and consistent.

> YOU ARE THE BEST PROJECT YOU CAN EVER WORK ON.

The Power of Gratitude

A lot can be said for having an attitude of gratitude, but I have discovered that practicing gratitude has helped me clarify my purpose in life and made me a better person. It has made me more creative and fulfilled and as a creator, I don't know if I could be an effective influencer without tapping into the force of gratitude daily. And I definitely couldn't maintain my positive attitude, self-belief, and manifestation practices without it.

Your true creative work will always begin in your heart, at your center. If you're opening Instagram to write a post and feeling immediately stuck creatively, it's because you haven't taken the time first to connect to your heart. I am way sharper, more creative, and a better servant when I take time to begin my day with a positive thought and a grateful heart. Gratitude is the fuel for creativity as gas is the fuel that makes the car go. Don't forget to fill up! As influencers, we are always in the pursuit of our dreams and goals. So much of what is out there teaches us that purpose is mostly a function of doing and producing, but seldom teaches that our purpose is also a function of being and appreciating. Our culture has a way of reminding us that we are not where we want to be in our lives yet. We are constantly focussing on the gap between where we are and where we want to be. But when you realize that it's what you do with that gap that is the most crucial, you'll realize your true power. It would be my suggestion that you fill that gap with gratitude. If you try to fill it with more doing, producing, or chasing success, you are never going to feel like you are making progress. As we seek to create more influence in the world, we have to remember the words of Jim Rohn; *"Learn how to be happy with what you have while you pursue all that you want."* That's amazing advice! One of the most important lessons we can learn in life is to be thankful for what we have been blessed with and what we have accomplished so far. You may not be where you want to be, but be grateful that you are not where you used to be. My life has taught me this valuable lesson of how gratitude and our purpose are connected. The more gratitude I give for the opportunities to use my influence big or small, the more the universe opens doors to me. When you start expressing gratitude for what you have and see it as part of your purpose, the windows of blessings will open up to you and miracles will begin to flow your way.

It has been observed in the scientific community that people who live a life of gratitude are more creative than people who don't. Here is what the HeartMath Institute says about this connection; *"The greater your capacity for sincere appreciation, the deeper the connection to your heart, where intuition and unlimited inspiration and possibilities reside."*

> WE ARE CONSTANTLY FOCUSSING ON THE GAP BETWEEN WHERE WE ARE AND WHERE WE WANT TO BE. BUT WHEN YOU REALIZE THAT IT'S WHAT YOU DO WITH THAT GAP THAT IS THE MOST CRUCIAL, YOU'LL REALIZE YOUR TRUE POWER.

When I am in a grateful, calm, and happy state, I always notice a boost in my creativity. When we are stressed, anxious, depressed, or tired, we are out of creative alignment and we feel stuck. It's hard to be grateful and stressed at the same time. It's also hard to reach our creative potential without gratitude. Gratitude shifts our energy and our thoughts into a more positive state. Practicing gratitude gets you in the habit of putting your focus on something outside the problem in front of you. Being a creator and a purpose-driven influencer doesn't give you a pass on life's problems. You'll still have bills, crises, distractions, issues in your love life and your career, etc. I know for me, it's hard to produce when life is coming at me fast. We have to cultivate the ability to be grateful so we can be creative. By cultivating this ability to be grateful, we are training our minds to always focus on the good no matter what is happening around us, because we know it's about what is happening within us. This is what gives you the resilience and self-awareness to weather the storm and keep your frequency high enough to appreciate the lessons the storm is providing you with. You never receive more than you can currently handle, sometimes what appears to be a crisis is actually preparing you for your manifestation to come to fruition. Gratitude will keep you on the right path as you expand into who you need to be to receive what you want.

Take Action:

On my nightstand, there is a sign that says; *"I Am Grateful."* That is the first thing I see when I wake up and the last thing I see when I go to bed. Placing that sign there was intentional. I wanted a visual reminder that would help me to remember to always practice gratitude. Earlier in the chapter, we discussed gratitude as part of your PDI routine, and if you haven't yet implemented it, now is the time. If you have, let's uplevel it. You can never have too much gratitude! I personally prefer to speak my gratitude out loud, because when you do, you're speaking into existence more of the good you want to multiply in your life. As a result of that, you are also letting the words and thoughts seep into your subconscious mind. Here's what I want you to do:

1. Place visual reminders of gratitude in your space. That can be in the form of a sticky note on the bathroom mirror that reads; *"I am grateful for my life"*. It could be keeping your gratitude journal by your bed, or labeling your alarm as; *"Wake up with gratitude"*. If you create an atmosphere of gratitude around you, you will always have gratitude within you.

2. Be Gratitude conscious. Life is filled with tiny miracles daily, it takes awareness to notice them. Start your day by searching for small things in your life to be grateful for. I know life comes with its challenges and at times gratitude might be the furthest thing from your mind, but if you wake up every day looking for everything right with your life instead of everything that is wrong with it, you will realize how blessed you are in spite of what is happening around you. There is a quote by Ghandi that helps me to keep things in proper perspective. He said; *"I was sad because I had no shoes, until I met a man who had no feet."* At times, we get so lost in our problems that we lose our ability to see the daily miracles. This quote will remind you to appreciate what you have because someone always has it worse than we do. I always say, if you have life, you have purpose. Therefore, you have something to be grateful for. The beat of your heart is a gift. The breath in your lungs is a gift. Your ability to read this book right now is a gift. Begin by focusing on the small blessings. Express gratitude for great weather, for the book you're reading, the person who held the door open for you, the person who packed your groceries at the supermarket, and for the free upgrade on your vacation.

3. Connect deeply to gratitude. Don't just go through the motions by speaking a bunch of words that are not connected to your heart. Real gratitude is deeper than a list of things you've written down or the words that are coming out of your mouth. Instead of saying I'm grateful for a

roof over my head and moving on to the next thing, ask yourself WHY are you grateful for the roof over your head? Also, think about what life would be if you did not have the things you are expressing gratitude for. The thought of no longer having a home, food to eat, good people in your life, or your health, is a powerful way to engage your emotions during your gratitude time. You will feel a deeper connection and appreciation for what you have.

4. Practice gratitude in advance. My favorite part of my gratitude practice is when I get to say thank you for the things that I don't have in my life yet to my creator. This is where I get to have so much fun with my gratitude practice. Neal Donald Walsh said; *"Gratitude in advance is the most powerful creative force in the universe"*. Once I learned gratitude in advance, it changed my life and the energy I show up in the world with, especially in how I pray. My prayers went from begging God, the universe, to coming from a place of assurance. My prayers used to consist of, help me God, I need you, I need a miracle, a breakthrough, bless me with money. These types of prayers leave you feeling empty and with no peace of mind afterward. It feels like your prayers are just hitting the ceiling. There is a way to fix that. Simply start by saying thank you, God, loving universe, for wisdom, for my new job with the perfect salary, thank you for my breakthrough that is already in motion, thank you for success and oppor-

tunities, thank you for a loving relationship, thank you that all my needs are met. This is the difference between prayers of desperation and prayers of realization. Express gratitude in advance for what you want as if you already know abundance and blessings are your birthright. Don't wait for things to happen, start expressing gratitude in advance and watch how your blessings get activated.

5. Practice constant gratitude. In moments when you're doing trivial things like washing the dishes, cleaning the house, or commuting to work, start speaking out loud what you are grateful for, or say it under your breath if you are around people. Being in a constant state of gratitude makes it harder for you to focus on the negative when you are consistently creating joy and good vibes.

Gratitude is more than an attitude, it's an action. When you take the time to practice gratitude intentionally every day, a grateful mindset will become a habit.

The Purpose-Driven Influencer Pledge

As we reach the end of this book and our journey together, I have one more thing to ask of you. It is my sincere hope that I have served you in all the ways that are necessary for your next steps in following a life and career of purpose and impact. My goal in writing this book was to provide influencers with the wisdom and resources to create true and lasting impact in the world, in all the ways that are personally resonant for you. It is a far from easy road, but I hope you have discovered the tools in this book that will support and ground you along the way. You will not be perfect, and you shouldn't aim to be. You will not be without days in which you feel completely disconnected from your purpose, and that's completely normal. You will face challenges, setbacks, and disappointments, they're all to be expected. But, you are a purpose-driven influencer, and you are bigger, bolder, and wiser than it all. Be grateful for it all. Actively seek the wisdom in it all. Remember your why and remember that you are walking this path of purpose because it is your destiny. I have one final action for you to take before our time together comes to a close. I want you to take the purpose-driven influencer pledge with me. You will find this below. You can take a picture of it with your phone, you can copy it out in handwriting, or you can type it out and print it. But I want you to have a physical copy of it other than the last page of this book. I want it to be somewhere accessible for you at all times so that when you face those challenges, you have a light guiding you th rough.

We are purpose-driven influencers. We seek to serve. We exist to create impact. And we achieve our goals with a happy smile and a grateful heart because we live to show what is possible and how beautiful this world can be when you are led by purpose.

Here is our pledge:

I, [   ], pledge to use my influence with purpose and integrity. I commit to sharing my truth, uplifting others, and creating a positive impact. My platform will be a space for inspiration, service, and positive change. I will lead with authenticity, prioritize purpose over popularity, and contribute to a better world through my influence. This is my commitment as a Purpose-Driven Influencer.

It has been a privilege to share this wisdom with you and I thank you for taking the time to sit with my book. We are now a part of each other's journey, and this is something I do not take lightly. I am so grateful for your trust. Now it's time for you to go out into the world and make your mark as a purpose-driven influencer. Don't be a stranger along the way! Send me a message sometime and let me know how you're getting on. It would be one of my greatest honors to witness you in your greatness.

Congratulations on reaching the end of this transformative journey. As you close this book, remember, this isn't the end—it's a new beginning. You've delved into the depths of authenticity, service, identity, and purposeful influence. Your heart is now aligned with your intentions, ready to illuminate the digital landscape and the world with your unique light.

I want you to take a moment and recognize the growth within you. You've embraced the power of your voice, learned to navigate the sometimes tricky waters of social media, and discovered the importance of leading from the heart. But this journey doesn't conclude here; it merely opens the door to a more profound expedition.

As you step forward, keep your authenticity as your compass and your purpose as your guiding star. Continue to influence with integrity, using your digital platform as a force for good. Your story is still unfolding, and each post, video, message, or encounter is a chance to impact lives positively.

Remember, leading with alignment is a daily practice, not a destination. Cherish the path you've created, embrace the passion that fuels your purpose, and always let your heart guide your influence. The world needs your unique voice, your genuine presence, and your heart-led leadership.

Thank you for embarking on this journey with me. Your purpose-driven influence is a gift to the world, and I can't wait to witness the incredible impact you're destined to make.

With heartfelt gratitude and excitement for what lies ahead,

Jimmy Jean

A Moment Of Gratitude

I extend my deepest gratitude to God for illuminating my path with the divine idea and inspiration to bring "The Purpose-Driven Influencer" to life. This journey would not be possible without His guidance.

To my beloved wife, Charanna Alexander Jean, your unwavering love and support are the cornerstones of this dream-turned-reality. Thank you for being my anchor, pushing me on days I hesitated to show up. You are not just my life partner, you are my purpose partner. I love you immensely.

My little one, AJ, though still a baby, your presence ignites a fire within me to become the best version of myself. Thank you for being a driving force behind Daddy's pursuit of greatness.

To my mother, Yanick Jean, you were my first example of a Purpose-Driven Influencer. Your selfless acts and dedication to helping others have shaped my understanding that life is about extending a hand to those in need.

Heartfelt thanks to my grandmother, Jeanine Brice, and aunt, Chantel Brice, who are both integral parts of the village that raised me. Your love and guidance continue to be a source of strength.

To my second grandma, Eleonore, who is no longer with us, but always in spirit. Your eyes always lit up when I walked into the room. You always made me feel seen and special. Love you and miss you.

To my mother-in-law, Charmaine Alexander, thank you for your love and support.

To Rae Brown, thank you for your mentorship and for pushing me to be great.

To my incredible sisters, Sandy and Melissa, I am immensely proud of the journey we've walked together.

Lastly, a sincere appreciation to my mentor, Spencer Tillman, for your wisdom and unwavering encouragement. A big thank you to Mel Robbins for your impactful service to the world and for being a profound inspiration in my life.

Endnotes

1. Deepak Chopra. 1994. *"The Seven Spiritual Laws of Success"*. 99. Amber-Allen Publishing.

2. Norman Vincent, *The Power of Positive Thinking* (Prentice Hall, 1952), 11.